Kudzu Don't Cover Everything

Kudzu Don't Cover Everything

BO WHALEY

RUTLEDGE HILL PRESS
Nashville, Tennessee

Published in Nashville, Tennessee, by Rutledge Hill Press, Inc., 211 Seventh Avenue North, Nashville, TN 37219

Typography by D&T/Bailey Typography, Nashville, Tennessee

Library of Congress Cataloging-in-Publication Data

Whaley, Bo, 1926–
    Kudzu don't cover everything / Bo Whaley.
        p.   cm.
    ISBN 1-55853-260-9
    1. American wit and humor.   I. Title
PN6162.W456   1993
814'.54—dc20   93-6274
                                                               CIP

Printed in the United States of America
1 2 3 4 5 6 7 8 — 98 97 96 95 94 93

DEDICATION

To Henry Bowden, an outstanding attorney, a credit to his chosen profession, and a prolific writer.

Success has embraced him for more than fifty years, and he wears it well. Highly respected by his colleagues, at peace with himself, and loved by his multitude of friends, Henry Bowden is truly a man among men who would have succeeded in any profession he chose to enter.

But most of all, Henry is my friend . . . a good friend. For that I am proud.

SPECIAL ACKNOWLEDGMENT

To Kellye Elkins, the best (and prettiest) little typist in Georgia.

But for Kellye, I would still be using my patented PMC Typing Method (pick, miss, and cuss) in a desperate effort to meet my impatient, but understanding, publisher's deadline.

Kellye has the patience of Job, the strength of Samson (prior to his Delilah-arranged haircut), and the wit of Bombeck. She needs all three, in abundance, to work for me.

I love her.

CONTENTS

INTRODUCTION 9

PART 1: THE CLOSER I LOOK, THE MORE I SEE 17
The Thin Line between Truth and Fiction 19
I Like Things That Turn Out Right 21
Need a Few Good Excuses? 23
Excuses for Running Late 25
A Few Thoughts from the Road 27
Have You Ever Noticed? 29
Golf from a Fisherman's Point of View 31
Some People Live to Eat 33
Thoughts on "Word Stuff," Pondering 35
The Proper Dress Code for the Mall 37
Wisdom from South Georgia 39
Paradise on the Florida Coast 41

PART 2: LIFE NEVER CEASES TO AMAZE ME 43
Whatever Happened to Truth in Advertising? 45
Shopping Today Is an Adventure 47
Monday Is the Week's Worst 49
Questions! Questions! Very Irritating! 51
Hurricane Yuletide 53
The Height of Frustration 55
Vending Machine Frustration 57
Health Care Costs Aren't Funny, but They're a Joke 59
The Ridiculous Costs of Health Care 61
Can Anyone Out There Sing Our National Anthem? 63
This Is Football? 65
The Sports Card Craze Has Gone Crazy 69

PART 3: **THE GOOD OLD DAYS KEEP
GETTING BETTER** 71
Old Addictions Are Hard to Kick 73
The Phone Has Come a Long Way, or Has It? 75
Remember What It Was Like When? 77
How Cars Were Sold in the Good Old Days 79
For Those Born before 1945 81
A Backward Glance, Fifty Years Ago 83
Things Saved over the Years 85
Things Sure Have Changed in Thirty Years 87

PART 4: **IF WOMEN ARE THE OPPOSITE SEX,
WHAT ARE MEN?** 89
The Marriage Bomb Explodes 91
Mother Spills the Beans
on Daughter after Thirty Years 93
Housewife Takes Full Advantage of Opportunity 97
Dumb Blonde Joke Fad Has Fizzled Out 99
Equal Time for "Dumb Men" Jokes 101
Hall of Fame Housekeeper 103
Skippy and Superwomen 107
Caution: Compliment with Care 109
I'll Fall in Love at the Drop of a Pacifier 111
Laura 115

PART 5: **ANECDOTES AND BRAIN TWISTERS** 119
A Retort Is More Than Just a Reply 121
Classroom Humor 123
A Few Bits and Pieces 125
Doctors and Lawyers Are Good Targets 127
Good News, Bad News 129
Restaurant Talk 131
More Grin and Share It 133
Dublin's Great Storytellers 135
Good Jokes Don't Have to Be Dirty 137
A Few Words of Wisdom from Henry 141
The Art of Writing 143
Time to Put Old Gray Matter to Work 145

PART 6:   **POLITICS: THE BIGGEST JOKE OF ALL** 147
Let's Put the Working Class in Congress 149
Update on the Little Red Hen 151
A Few Ideas for Cutting the Deficit 153
Why I Will Never Run for President 155
I Want to Be King, Not President 157
Life on the Campaign Trail 159
Why My Vote Went to Bush 161
The Scoop from Shallow Throat 165
Shallow Throat Shows and Tells 167

PART 7:   **THOSE WHO SERVE** 169
Daddy's Notes 171
What Is a Farmer? 173
Putting Their Lives on the Line for You 175

INTRODUCTION

First off, thank you for buying this book. My banker thanks you, my ex-wife thanks you, the IRS thanks you, Southern Bell Telephone Company thanks you, Georgia Power Company thanks you, Cable TV Services thanks you, Ace Collection Service thanks you, American Express thanks you, Grange Insurance Company (auto) thanks you, Central Insurance Agency (home) thanks you, Prudential Insurance Company (health) thanks you, MasterCard thanks you, and so does VISA.

I feel duty-bound to enlighten you at the outset regarding the pros and cons of kudzu (pronounced "Cud-zoo") and, by so doing, shed some light on why I settled on the title of the book, *Kudzu Don't Cover Everything*.

As a newspaper columnist since 1978, I realize and appreciate the excellent coverage afforded national and world events by the media. Like the Persian Gulf War, for instance. When was the last time you sat in your recliner and watched a war from the comfort and safety of your den? Cable News Network (CNN) did an outstanding job reporting the conflict. Likewise with NBC, CBS, ABC, the Associated Press (AP), International News Service (INS), the nation's newspapers, and radio. Not to mention the local bars, coffee shops, barbershops, and beauty shops.

But, like kudzu, they don't cover everything. They try, but it's not possible. There is too much going on in the world.

I wrote this book in an attempt to cover some of the things the media either missed or overlooked and kudzu couldn't get to—like some of the finer points of the 1992 presidential election campaigns of George Bush and Bill Clinton; when to and how to compliment women, and when to refrain from doing so; what to wear to be in vogue when mall shopping; why I will never run for president; the ups and downs of farmers and preachers; frustration caused by vending machines; a thumbnail sketch of the medical profession; the thin line between truth and fiction; superwomen; the joy of being in love; football as it is today; the crazy sports card craze; and more than sixty other topics the media didn't cover.

I urge you, now that you have invested $5.95 of your hard-earned money on it, to keep this book in a safe place. Guard and protect it, lend it to friends and neighbors with care, and get a receipt. Never leave it unattended in a car, a coffee shop, a bar, on a park bench or in a hospital waiting room. Do so and it could disappear, and you might never see it again.

Be especially protective of it because you never know—one day it may be worth $5.95.

Now . . . The Pros and Cons of Kudzu

If you have read this far, there is a good chance that you have already asked yourself, "What the heck is kudzu?" No problem. I anticipated that. That's the very reason I conducted in-depth and far reaching research into the subject.

My first assigned task in an effort to get the straight skinny on kudzu was to contact a great friend, a fellow author and radio talk-show host, Ludlow Porch, who hangs his hat on a microphone in Atlanta, Georgia, and writes books in his mountain cabin in North Georgia near Amicalola Falls, sitting in the middle of a scene painted by God.

I did this because Ludlow knows almost everything there is to know about almost everything, including kudzu. He's also my best friend. I respect his knowledge. He has been named by *Sports Illustrated* magazine as one of the five recognized trivia experts in the world.

Ludlow knows more about trivia than Albert Einstein knew about long division; more about "The Andy Griffith Show" than Don Knotts, Gomer Pyle, Opie, and Aunt Bee combined; more about old movies than Laurel and Hardy; more about dancing than Arthur Murray; more about old television shows than Milton Berle and Sid Caesar; more about sports than Howard Cosell; and more about grits than Aunt Jemima.

I knew he would know about kudzu. This is what he told me about it:

I don't know how many acres of land in the South have been taken over by kudzu, but it must be in the millions. It covers the shoulders of roads, old farmhouses, abandoned cars, and just about everything else.

There seems to be no way to kill kudzu. It is tougher than a ten-cent steak, and no matter how you fight it, kudzu always seems to come out the winner.

Here's a true account of how kudzu came to our beloved South-land, as well as the shocking answer to one of this nation's most baffling mysteries:

Kudzu was originally brought to America by a Japanese gentleman named Herschell Lamar Kudzu, a seed salesman from Tokyo. Old Herschell convinced some farmers that they could plant kudzu and use it as cattle feed, but he explained to them that kudzu could grow faster than the cattle could eat it. What he didn't tell them, however, was that kudzu could also grow faster than a grown man could run. His pitch was successful, and kudzu was planted all over the South.

Now, one of the great unsolved mysteries concerns Amelia Earhart's disappearance. Oldtimers, however, know the truth. Just before she was supposed to take off on her around-the-world trip, she walked out on the edge of a kudzu field to take a whiz. It was a horrible thing to watch. The kudzu got her, it got her airplane, it also got a midget who was playing "Lady of Spain" on a little biddy accordion. Neither has been seen or heard from since.

You see, what Herschell Lamar didn't tell anybody was that cows don't eat kudzu, but kudzu will flat eat a cow.

And that's what Ludlow says about kudzu.

I wanted a second opinion, just to be sure, so I contacted another friend, Paul Riddle, a bigwig with the University of Georgia Cooperative Extension Service. I explained my interest in kudzu; and within a matter of a few days he sent me the following information, which, if you're to become a kudzu expert, you must know and understand. This research paper was prepared by Dr. A. E. Smith, a professor of agronomy at the

University of Georgia College of Agriculture Experiment Station, Griffin, Georgia:

> Kudzu (*Pueraria lobata*) is a vigorously growing perennial vine belonging to the legume family. It has a well developed root system that exceeds the mass of foliage produced by the plant.
>
> Kudzu, a native of China, was introduced into the United States in 1876. It was originally cultured as a foliage crop and for stabilization of highly erodible land in the southeastern United States. It has a prolific growth rate, which limits man's ability to restrict its invasion into contiguous areas. Additionally, kudzu does not tolerate intensive grazing and haying practices. Therefore, kudzu has lost its importance as a forage crop and is presently considered a weed in forests, pastures, and rights-of-way.
>
> Kudzu has infested thousands of acres of forest land and roadsides in the southeastern United States and is considered an economically important pest. It grows in tree canopies, on the ground, and over buildings.

And that's what Dr. Smith has to say about kudzu, about the same as Ludlow but in university language.

Conclusion: Kudzu grows faster than a runaway husband can run, covers everything in sight, and can't be controlled.

I grew up in the South and was on a first-name basis with kudzu for years, until I moved to snow country. Like sore eyes, stumped toes, mumps, and measles, I just figured it was something to be put up with.

Now, years later, I have certain opinions, like other natives of the South, about kudzu and what it can do and has done in the past. Some folks, including me, are pretty well convinced that kudzu was responsible for some pretty notable events down through the years. There is no other explanation for these happenings:

• Kudzu got Jimmy Hoffa. He was kidnapped in Michigan and while being transported to Florida by a few hoods he jumped out of the big, black limousine near Waycross, Georgia, landed in a kudzu field, and hasn't been heard from since.

• Kudzu swallowed up "The Lost Chord." It was written on a separate sheet of tablet paper, the last sheet, and blew off the piano back in the 1920s when Miss Bessie Rigdon was playing a piano recital out from Ludowici, Georgia, in Mount Zion Church. The church wasn't air-conditioned, the windows were up, and "The Lost Chord" blew out of the window and landed in a nearby kudzu field—lost forever.

• Kudzu was also responsible for the disappearance of the sheep that was lost in Matthew 18:12 and found in Matthew 18:13. A giant field of kudzu just engulfed that little sheep, separating it from the other ninety-nine, and kept it for two verses.

• Kudzu also played a bad trick on Little Bo Peep. Remember? "Little Bo Peep has lost her sheep and doesn't know where to find them." All Little Bo had to do was search the nearest kudzu field. She would have found 'em right off.

• Kudzu even invades the world of literature now and then and has been doing it since at least 1933 when James Hilton wrote his novel *Lost Horizon,* which became the first paperback book issued by Pocket Books in 1939 and sold for twenty-five cents. Hilton's horizon wasn't lost; kudzu climbed on the rainbow, spread to its end, and once there, grabbed it.

While it is not general knowledge, I have it on good authority from "Booger" Edwards, who lives in a tree house by the Altamaha River near Uvalda, Georgia, that kudzu has also been responsible for the disappearance of other American legends. Like:

• Hadacol. Kudzu got it. You *know* Colonel LeBlanc wouldn't have voluntarily given up such a gold mine.

• Hoola-hoops. Same. There are millions of the things covered in some giant kudzu field in South Georgia just waiting to be shook.

• Davy Crockett coonskin caps. Gone the kudzu route.

And more . . . watch pockets, zoot suits (thank goodness), marbles, milk churns, tuning forks, porches, feather beds, automobile spotlights, nonfilter cigarettes, knickers (thank goodness), decent movies, real milk shakes, stick matches, and Cokes in six-ounce bottles. Gone. Kudzu victims, I'm convinced of it.

Kudzu is a killer weed. Now you know.

*   *   *

As I write, I can't help but put myself in the reader's shoes and consider the story of the little boy who asked his daddy after supper one night as he was doing his homework, "Daddy, would you tell me a little bit about penguins?"

"Go ask your mother," the daddy said without bothering to look up from his newspaper.

"No, thanks, I don't wanna know that much about 'em."

So the daddy drops his newspaper, puts on his coat, and says to the boy, "Come with me. I'm tired of having to do all your homework. This time, you're gonna do it."

He took his son to the library, checked out five books on penguins, and returned home.

"Now, go to your room and read all five of those books before you come out," he commanded.

Several hours later the boy, tired and sleepy, stumbled into the den.

"You read all of 'em?" his daddy asked.

"Yes, sir."

"You learn anything about penguins?"

"Yes, sir," the boy replied. "I learned a heck of a lot more about 'em than I ever wanted to know."

Take heart. Keep the faith. Remember this: While kudzu *is* a pest, it don't cover everything.

Kudzu Don't Cover Everything

ANTHEM OF THE KUDZU
By Vern F. Highley

The Kudzu vines are marching
They've formed a mighty throng
Moving out of Memphis and all points South
Singing the "Kudzu Song"

Tha-rumpa, tha-rumpa
Tha-rumpa-rumpa-doo
That's the sound and cadence
Of the Mighty Kudzu

They're marching through the Southland
Marching through the day and all night
Leaving no path or roadside fallow
Climbing every telephone pole in sight

Tha-rumpa, tha-rumpa
Tha-rumpa-rumpa-doo
That's the sound and cadence
Of the Mighty Kudzu

Their winding, binding vines
Decorate the hillside scene
Where the landscape once was barren
It's now a Kudzu green

Tha-rumpa, tha-rumpa
Tha-rumpa-rumpa-doo
That's the sound and cadence
Of the Mighty Kudzu

They've many miles to cover
To the Gulf and Atlantic shore
Once they reach the water
They'll turn around and march some more

Tha-rumpa, tha-rumpa
Tha-rumpa-rumpa-doo
That's the sound and cadence
Of the Mighty Kudzu

Editor's note: Mr. Highley specializes in government relations in Washington, DC for agricultural interests. While driving to a meeting in Mississippi several years ago, he became intrigued with the Kudzu and wrote these lyrics to a song. "Like the Kudzu," Highley says, "this song goes on and on." Used with permission.

PART ONE

THE CLOSER I LOOK, THE MORE I SEE

While I doubt that he ever really said it, Yogi Berra is credited with having said, "You can observe a lot by just watching."

On the other hand, I harbor no doubt that television comedian "Flip" Wilson said, "What you see is what you get." I know he said it, many times. I saw and heard him. It is the statement with which he is probably most closely identified.

I particularly like the story that made the rounds regarding a celebrated court case in South Georgia in which a man was being tried on an aggravated assault charge. Specifically, he was charged with having bitten the ear off a patron in a juke joint when they got into a nasty fight over a bar waitress.

The story goes that the juke joint's eighty-two-year-old janitor, Clem Barron, was subpoenaed to testify as a prosecution witness as Clem reportedly was the only witness to the ear-biting episode.

Clem was sworn in, took a seat in the witness chair, and readied himself for questioning by the district attorney, a petite and cocksure little lawyer with a chip on his shoulder the size of a bale of cotton. He had not lost a case in three years, and, as they say in South Georgia, "He was feeling his oats."

"You do realize, don't you, Mr. Barron, that you are under oath to tell the truth?" the DA asked.

"Yessuh', I do," Clem answered.

"All right. Then tell the court where you were on the night of July 10, 1987, at approximately 2:00 A.M."

"I wuz in th' Bottoms Up Bar on Shady Lane, in Coogan, Georgia," Clem said.

"And precisely what were you doing there at that hour?"

"I wuz moppin' th' floor an' cleanin' up."

"You work there, do you?"

"Yessuh. Been workin' there f'r nine years. I'm th' janitor."

"All right, now tell the court. Did you witness an altercation between the victim and the accused?"

"Witness a whut, sir?"

"A fight. Did you see a fight between Jack Croaker, the victim, and Roscoe Bailey, the defendant in this case?"

"Oh, a fight! Yessuh, I seen 'em fightin', I sho' did."

"All right. Now then, I have but one question for you, sir. Now think before you answer because your reply is vitally important to this case. And I caution you to remember that you are under oath. The question: Did you, or did you not, see with your own eyes Roscoe Bailey bite Jack Croaker's ear off?"

Silence filled the courtroom as old Clem pondered the question. The judge leaned forward, joining the jury in anticipation of Clem's answer. Roscoe Bailey fidgeted and squirmed in his chair at the defense table.

Finally, Clem cleared his throat and said, "Nossir, I can't rightly say that I seen Roscoe bite Jack's ear off."

"No further questions of this witness, Your Honor," the little DA said haughtily and with an air of disgust turned and walked back toward his chair at the prosecutor's table.

Just as the prosecutor started to sit down, Clem continued with his statement from the witness chair, "But . . . I seen him spit it out!"

Like Yogi, Flip, and old Clem, I am an observer, and I record what I observe. It is not always what I see that I record, but through the years of writing I have learned that the closer I look, the more I see.

That is what I've done in this section of this book. I have observed and written about things like golf from a fisherman's viewpoint, proper dress codes for the shopping mall, a paradise on the Florida coast, and things that turn out right, among others.

THE THIN LINE BETWEEN TRUTH AND FICTION

There is a thin line between truth and fiction. A good example of this can be heard every year during the Masters golf tournament:

Fiction: "Nah, I decided not to go this year. You see one Masters you've seen 'em all. I'd rather stay home and watch it on television."

Truth: He had no tickets although he made 327 telephone calls trying to find some. He offered to drive to New Jersey if necessary to come up with tickets. He ran an ad in the newspaper and on the radio and would gladly have paid $200 per ticket.

I've collected lots of other examples.

Fiction: "No way am I going to vote in this year's election with what we have to choose from."

Truth: At 7:05 A.M., he's at the polling place and can hardly wait to get into the voting booth. He would have been there earlier but he stopped to put a bumper sticker on his car that reads "Vote For Blowhard—A Proven Winner."

Fiction: "Who, Connie? Man, I wouldn't take her to the office Christmas party if you paid me to do it. I'll admit she looks good, but she ain't too smart. Know what I mean?"

Truth: He started in January asking Connie to go with him to the party. He asked every week, sent flowers and candy regularly. Connie turned him down every time.

Fiction: I'm thinking about cashing in all my CDs and putting the money in Treasury notes. The interest on the CDs is way too low. I can do better with my money."

Truth: The only notes he has are for two loans, both overdue. His checking account is getting close to the red border, and a deposit is needed immediately.

Fiction: "Yeah, I played professional baseball for five years. I quit when I wasn't brought up to the majors after having two great seasons in a row. I even led the league one year."

Truth: He played for five years. That's true. He neglected to point out that his batting averages were .139, .181, .202, .144, and .176. He did lead the league one year—in broken bats and stolen towels.

Fiction: "No, thank you. I wouldn't have one of those cars if you gave it to me. Nothing but trouble."

Truth: He has a 1965 Plymouth and a 1969 Chevrolet. It's a miracle when both are running on the same day. His most valuable accessory is a set of jumper cables.

Fiction: "Oh, yeah. I've already decided. This year I'm either gonna take the family to Panama City, the Bahamas, or Disney World. I may fly and take 'em to all three."

Truth: What he did was load the family up and take 'em to Jaybird Springs for a day and for a picnic on Turkey Creek. And he didn't fly, he drove.

Fiction: "Man, I've got the best fishing hole around. I caught sixteen there yesterday. I'd be glad to tell you where it is, but I promised the owner I wouldn't."

Truth: He caught sixteen all right—three stumps, two old shoes, three tin cans, two turtles, four limbs, and two fish about the size of a small pocketknife.

Fiction: "Did I eat 'em up? Man, I hadn't been in Las Vegas more than ten minutes when I hit a $1,000 jackpot on a slot machine. I went on to win $1,200 at blackjack and another $1,500 on the roulette wheel. That was just the first night. The next day I stuck with the crap tables and doubled my money. I started not to come home."

Truth: He started not to come home, that's for sure. He lost his return air fare and had to wire his mama to send him $350 to get home on.

I LIKE THINGS THAT TURN OUT RIGHT

I like things that turn out right, like World War II, for instance. I thought the ending was really neat. But I'll admit there are times when I question who won, like when I consider things like economics and trade deficits.

You remember World War II, don't you? That's the one in which both Italy and France drew byes and Japan, Germany, Russia, and the United States ended up in the Final Four.

Italy threw up its hands and surrendered when the first tank backfired.

The biggest sale on army rifles in history was held in Paris early in 1946 when hundreds of thousands of them were offered for sale. This sign advertised it: "French Army rifles for sale. Never been fired—and only dropped once."

So much for World War II. All's well that ends well.

Like I said, I like things that end right, but *Gone With the Wind* ain't one of 'em. I never look at the movie, which airs at least once a year on television. On each occasion the end result is the same: we lose. I ain't gonna' watch it until they run it backward so it ends right.

The same with the book. I've read it several times. The South always loses. So does Scarlett, and rightfully so.

Then there's the matter of the 1992 presidential election. I don't know if it turned out right or not. Let's hope and pray that it did. Only time will tell if a woman president can cut the mustard.

In spite of all this, many things do turn out right. Here's an example of one that did:

One of my best friends confided in me last week that a tumor (a lump) had been found in his wife's breast. Naturally, he was much concerned.

A few days later he was all smiles. Earlier in the day he had received the results of the biopsy—benign.

What a beautiful word *benign* is! It's music, sweet music, to the ears.

Here are some of the things I definitely like:

• I like it when final examinations turn out right, and everybody passes.

• I like it when bank balances turn out right, in the black.

• I like it when breakfast turns out right and the eggs, sausage, grits, toast, and coffee are cooked to perfection, and the waitress is happy and cheerful.

• I like it when automobile repairs turn out right after pulling into a repair shop with a coughing engine and visions of a sky-high repair bill and the mechanic smiles and says, "Just a loose spark plug wire. No charge."

• I like it when telephone calls turn out right and the late night caller says, "I just wanted to say hello. Haven't talked to you in a while and wanted to find out if all is well with you."

• I like it when Form 1040s turn out right and on April 16th I still have enough money left for a hamburger.

• I like it when a child's birthday party turns out right, and even more when I arrive home after a hard day of loafing and find this note in my door from a pretty nine-year-old girl:

To: Mr. Whaley
Thank you for the birthday card and the five dollars. Also, thank you for writing about me in the paper.
But even more, thank you for being my friend.
Love,
Kaylie Sellers

• I like it when golf drives turn out right, and any drive I hit turns out right when it stays in the fairway.

• I like it when tornado warnings for Middle Georgia turn out right, and they're canceled.

• I like it when open heart surgery turns out right, it "keeps on ticking," and the news is progressively good that Lewis Grizzard is on the way back to his typewriter. Remember the boy in your prayers . . . again.

NEED A FEW GOOD EXCUSES?

The 1992 election is history, thankfully. Hopefully, we will survive as a nation under the reign of His Royal Highness King William I of the House of Clinton, who succeeded to the throne January 20, 1993, and Her Royal Hindness Princess Hillary who, to paraphrase Sen. Lloyd Bentsen's comeback remark to Vice President Dan Quayle in a 1988 debate, "is no Princess Diana."

This chapter is about employee responsibility, or the lack of it. The subject came to mind on Saturday when I visited a television station in Atlanta and saw a small plaque on a wall in the employees' lounge. I read it twice. Then I reached for pad and pen and recorded these words from it:

Attention All Employees

In order to save time, please give excuses by the numbers corresponding with the excuses listed below. In so doing this office should operate in a much more efficient manner by affording more time to our employees for such things as personal telephone calls, visits to the rest rooms, nail polishing, office pools on sporting events, girl and boy watching, as well as the inevitable gossip sessions that occur in the hallways.

Your cooperation in this matter is earnestly solicited and will be sincerely appreciated.

1. The computer fouled it up.
2. I didn't think it was all that important.
3. Don't blame me. I was hired for my looks.
4. That's not my department.
5. No one told me to go ahead with it.
6. I've been too busy.
7. We've always done it this way.
8. I forgot.
9. I was waiting for the OK.

10. That's someone else's job.
11. My supervisor didn't tell me.
12. I was out sick and missed the briefing.
13. I thought the deadline was tomorrow.
14. I forgot that this is Leap Year and there are 29 days in February.
15. I goofed!

(OTHER: Please fill in the blank: _____)

Excuses can be handy tools when used properly. Like the story of the South Georgia farmer who was approached by a neighbor whom he didn't particularly like who asked to borrow a rope.

The farmer refused with the excuse that he had only one rope and had used it to tie up flour.

"But it is impossible to tie up flour with a rope," the borrower protested.

Undaunted, the farmer said to him, "I can tie up anything with a rope if I don't want to lend it."

Probably one of the most well-known excuses came from the television series "Chico and the Man" that aired several years ago. The show left the air following the suicide death of the star, Freddie Prinz, only twenty-two, who played "Chico." Maybe you remember Chico's catch phrase to the old man when he didn't want to perform a chore: "That's no my job, man."

By far the best excuse I've ever heard came from Dublin's premier teller of tales, G. C. Hawkins. His good friend, Grady Cullens, swears this story is true:

The two of them were fishing near Blackshear's Ferry one Sunday morning when the bell of Marie Church began to ring. Grady asked of his fishing buddy, "G. C., don't you think we really ought to be in church instead of out here fishing?"

G. C., while rebaiting his hook, replied, "Naw, I couldn't a' gone anyway."

"Why not?" asked Grady.

Without looking up, G. C. said, "My wife's sick."

EXCUSES FOR RUNNING LATE

Is there anything more frustrating than a person who habitually runs late? I had a roommate in college who was undoubtedly programmed to run late. He was even late for his graduation. The guy would know he had to be somewhere at 8:00 P.M., yet he wouldn't even begin to dress until about 8:30 P.M.

Even weirder than people who regularly run late are the excuses they offer. If you are one of those who can't seem to arrive anywhere on time, I have a list of excuses for you:

Sorry, I'm late but:

- My hair dryer broke.
- I forgot to set my clock.
- My parakeet died.
- My mother called.
- I saw an injured puppy along the road and took it to the vet.
- I lost my keys.
- My boss called and asked me to run by and feed his cat.
- I had to stop for gas and a tuneup.
- A bill collector came to the door, and I hid until he left.
- I tried to swerve, but I saw the bus too late.
- I dropped one of my contact lenses down the sink and had to call a plumber.
- My cat had kittens.
- I made cookies for you but I burned them.
- A movie was being filmed on the corner and they had the street blocked.
- A friend called and said she was contemplating suicide.
- I spilled plant food on my clothes.
- I didn't know we were still on Eastern Standard Time.
- I locked my keys in my car.
- I took a shortcut, and you won't believe how lost I got.
- A heel came off my shoe.
- A mad dog came and sat

in my driveway.

- I wanted to look so good for you that I couldn't make up my mind what to wear.
- I bit into a peanut, a filling came out, and I had to go by my dentist.
- I had a flat tire and didn't have the slightest idea how to go about changing it.
- After a nice man changed my tire, my battery died.
- My toilet wouldn't stop flushing.
- My zipper got stuck in the down position.
- My hot curlers blew a fuse.
- Dialing for Dollars called.
- Just as I walked outside to come to work you wouldn't believe the lightning.
- The traffic was awful.
- I didn't realize today was Wednesday.
- I couldn't find a parking place.
- I felt real dizzy. I think I may be pregnant.
- My daughter left home without lunch money, and I had to run by the school.
- A vegetable truck overturned right in front of me.
- My bathtub faucet stuck in the on position.
- My sister called just as I was walking out of the house.
- My aunt called after my sister hung up.
- I didn't know there was going to be a bus strike.
- A homeless person came begging at my door and I fed him.
- I had to mail in my income tax. Today is the last day and I didn't have a stamp, so I had to go to the post office.
- One of my neighbor's big oak trees fell across my driveway.
- Some man with a religious group rang my doorbell and tried to sell me a book.
- UPS arrived with the set of encyclopedias I ordered. They were shipped C.O.D., and I couldn't find my pocketbook.
- The state patrol was conducting a driver's license and proof of insurance inspection. There was a long line. I found my driver's license right off but had a hard time finding my insurance card that was buried in my glove compartment.

A FEW THOUGHTS FROM THE ROAD

I picked up or conjured up these thoughts while traveling around the country.

• It is certainly not necessary to drink to be a good columnist. It is a great help on the days when you are a bad one, however.

• Marriage teaches you loyalty, forbearance, self-restraint, meekness, thrift, and a great many other things you wouldn't need if you had stayed single.

• The surest way to make a red light turn green is to try and find something in the glove compartment.

• Change is inevitable, except from a vending machine.

• Intelligence is when you spot the flaw in your boss's reasoning. Wisdom is when you refrain from pointing it out.

• Two homeless drunks were sitting at the base of the Washington Monument on a bitter cold day in February. One started a fire at the base of the monument. The other said, "You'll never get it off the ground."

• Aren't the new cars ridiculous? There's one luxury car on the market now that is so modern and computerized that when you press a button *it* presses a button.

• A stunning young blonde walked into a dress shop and asked the manager, "Would you mind if I tried on that blue dress in the window?"

"Go right ahead," he said. "It might help business."

• Americans are getting stronger. Twenty-five years ago it took two people to carry fifty dollars worth of groceries. Today a five-year old can do it.

• I heard a great new song a couple of weeks ago, but it will never make it. I could understand every word.

• One day a fellow came home and found his new bride crying because her dog had eaten the pie she'd made especially for him. "Don't cry, honey," he said. "I'll buy you another dog."

- Things are still rough out there as evidenced by this note from a bank to a depositor: "This is to inform you that this is the last time this bank will spend twenty-nine cents to let you know you have twenty-eight cents."

- A poor guy married a liberated female, only to have her tell him after the ceremony that she didn't believe in sex after marriage.

- There's a new medical/legal TV show coming this fall. It's called "Perry Kildare" and filmed in Our Lady of Malpractice Hospital. The plot? It's about a lawyer who owns his own ambulance.

- The candidate said in his radio campaign ad: "My wife is the sweetest, most tolerant, most intelligent, most beautiful woman in the world. This is a paid political announcement."

- When I had dinner with WSB-Radio's laughable Ludlow Porch in Atlanta, the waiter said to him, "Just help yourself to the salad bar and fix your own salad." Ludlow countered with, "Certainly, I'll be glad to go to the salad bar and fix my own salad— provided you let me go behind the bar and fix my own martini."

- The elevator stops on the fifteenth floor and a nude woman steps into the elevator, occupied by a lone office worker, pushes the button for the fourth floor, and smiles sweetly.

Dumbfounded and not knowing just what to say, if anything, he finally says to her as they pass the sixth floor: "My wife has an outfit just like yours."

- Three cross-eyed prisoners appeared before a cross-eyed judge.

The cross-eyed judge turned to the first cross-eyed prisoner, and said, "What are you charged with?"

And the second cross-eyed prisoner said, "stealing chickens." The cross-eyed judge looked at him and said, "Keep quiet! I wasn't talking to you." And the third cross-eyed prisoner said, "I didn't say nothing."

HAVE YOU EVER NOTICED?

Some things we see are almost beyond belief.

I was returning to Dublin and stopped at a convenience store in Milledgeville for coffee. I get about eighteen miles to the cup on regular—twenty-two on decaffeinated.

As I was putting cream and sugar in my cup, a man walked in with a large Pepsi cup in his hand. He filled it with coffee. Then he repeatedly tore open little sugar packets and poured the contents into the coffee. Then, the nondairy creamers. I was amazed at the number of both he used.

I asked the clerk, "Do you have any idea how many sugars and creamers that fellow over there put in his coffee?"

Without hesitation, she said, "Yes, sixteen sugars and ten creamers. He comes in every morning and every afternoon for coffee. He always uses sixteen sugars and ten creamers."

I saw him do it. And I have a witness. She would verify it.

I'll bet he has a ball when he puts mustard and catsup on a hot dog or hamburger.

Have You Ever Noticed?

Many of us, myself included, often begin a statement with "Have you ever noticed?" Then we relate some observation we've made. Like these:

Have you ever noticed:

• One of the most difficult things in the world is to know how to do something and to watch, without comment, somebody else do it incorrectly.

• It doesn't start to get bumpy on an airplane until the flight attendant starts to serve the coffee.

• In America there are ten million laws to enforce the Ten Commandments.

• A man can say what he thinks in this country, provided he isn't afraid of his wife, his boss, his neighbors, his customers, or the government.

• You can complain because rose bushes have thorns, or you can rejoice

29

because thorn bushes have roses. It all depends on how you look at things.

● "In most cases on the job, if you aren't fired with enthusiasm, you'll be fired with enthusiasm."—Vince Lombardi.

● "An autobiography usually reveals nothing bad about its writer except his memory."—Franklin P. Jones.

● A lot of drivers don't need seat belts as much as they need straitjackets.

● A joint checking account is never overdrawn by the wife. It is just under-deposited by the husband.

● The average girl would much rather have beauty than brains because the average man can see much better than he can think.

● Some people will believe anything, if you whisper it.

● School days can be the happiest days of your life, provided your children are old enough to go.

● Some women show a lot of style, and some styles show a lot of women.

● No conversation is more boring than one where everybody agrees.

I recall a great statement by the late Sen. Everett Dirksen on the subject of anger. He said he had the greatest and wisest secretary in the world. When he dictated a letter in anger, she would not type it for twenty-four hours. Then, she would ask him, "Do you still want me to send that letter to So-and-So that you dictated yesterday?"

In most cases, Dirksen said, he would tell her to tear it up.

Dirksen's admission underscores this quote by the great philosopher Seneca: "The greatest remedy for anger is delay."

GOLF FROM A FISHERMAN'S POINT OF VIEW

Golfers and fishermen have had a friendly argument going on for years as to which is best.

- Lawyers play golf.
  Gen. Norman Schwarzkopf fishes.
- Golfers wear silly orange and pink slacks with no belt loops and pro shop shirts that cost a fortune.
  K-Mart is the only clothier a fisherman needs.
- Golfers wear special shoes with kinky names like Foot Joy and Etonic.
  Fishermen wear battered sneakers and thongs. Some even go barefoot.
- Televised golf is thick with British accents and Cadillac ads.
  Fishermen on TV talk like they're from Yulee, and the ads are for beer and chewing tobacco.
- Golf is hidebound by musty traditions, such as who has honors off the tee.
  When fishermen see a big swirl, there is no honor, only a scramble to be the first to cast.
- Golf is burdened by archaic rules drawn up in Scotland.
  Fishermen can learn the rules at Sleepy's Bait and Tackle.
- Golfers chew Doublemint.
  Fishermen chew Red Man.
- Golfers won't stoop to diving into a lake after a lost ball.
  A fisherman will step over cottonmouths to retrieve his favorite lure.
- Golfers complain that a 7:30 A.M. tee is too early.
  To a fisherman that's midmorning.
- Golfers go to a practice tee and practice before play begins.
  Fishermen don't need to practice. They're ready the minute they step out of the pickup.
- Golfers say it takes mental toughness to play golf, a de-

31

manding focus for eighteen holes, a cerebral analysis of each shot.

All it takes to fish is a can of worms.

- Fast-track business types hit the golf courses to unwind, then verbally abuse each other, throw and break clubs, and curse the heavens. This is not relaxation.

Fishermen get so laid back they sometimes fall asleep waiting for the rod or pole to bend.

- To a golfer, "hazards" are small patches of sand, quiet ponds and—this one's really frightening—trees.

Fishing hazards include capsizing, man-eating sharks, and snapping barracuda. You haven't lived until you've shared the cockpit of a small boat with a fish that doesn't want to be there.

- Golfers have names like Chip, Lance, Steve, and Ian.

Fishermen are Bubba, Earl, Bo, and Slick. And if you don't know another fisherman's name, just say "Hey, Bud," and you'll have made a friend.

- Golfers kill time by cleaning little pieces of sod from their spikes with a tee. (They wouldn't dare use their fingers.)

Fishermen kill time by probing for bits of Vienna sausage with a wooden match.

- The slightest disturbance—the click of a shutter or chirping of a bird—can upset a golfer's backswing, throwing him into a rage.

Fishermen sometimes bring radios with them.

- Golfers smell better, but fishermen hang out with other fishermen so it doesn't matter.

- Golfers yell "Fore" before beaning one of their own.

No such formality among fishermen. An errant cast is usually accompanied by "Watch out!" before the treble hooks lodge in your buddy's scalp.

- Fishermen come home with supper, a fresh seatrout or bass fillet.

A golfer's wife sends him to the supermarket for frozen cod from Newfoundland.

SOME PEOPLE LIVE TO EAT

"**S**ome people eat to live; other people live to eat."
I'm going to give you two examples of people who live to eat. Both are females.

I've always associated hearty appetites with males—like Japanese sumo wrestlers, NFL linemen, Roman emperors, and "Wimpy," the acknowledged king of hamburger eaters.

Females also come in for their share of culinary consumption, like two I know who would eat the bark off a sycamore tree and then look around for a small sapling for dessert.

What you are about to read is true. Only the names have been changed to protect me.

Debbie from Nashville

Debbie is lean and hungry. Debbie is always hungry. She is about 5'7", 115 pounds, with the figure of a model. In fact, she's been a model, a successful one. She's in her midthirties.

A few months ago I went to dinner with Debbie and her mother in Nashville. Debbie chose the restaurant, one of those exotic foreign jobs featuring dishes that are still growing, have no taste, and have price tags rivaling Neiman-Marcus sweaters. Patrons sit on the floor, barefoot. Any entree will melt an American Express Gold Card.

The maitre d' showed us to our table. It was cocktail time. I ordered a Coke, Debbie's mother a glass of white wine, and Debbie a concoction with a tropical name that had a palm tree growing out of it, which she promptly devoured upon finishing the drink.

Then came the menus. They resembled deed record books from the clerk of the court's office, and the prices would gag a giraffe. I fumbled through mine, unable to identify any item. Debbie's mother made a quick decision on page eleven. Debbie studied hers like a Rhodes scholar, muttering an occasional "Hmmmmmm . . . sounds great!" and said to no one in particular, "Lord! I'm hungry!" the understatement of the century.

Finally, Debbie made her choice.

"Have you decided?" the waiter asked.

"Yes," she said with a straight face, "I'll have page two, with butter."

I made a quick mental calculation of page two. Roughly $460, plus tax! I felt my Gold Card roll over and die.

Diana from Dublin

Diana is nineteen, petite, pretty, and hungry. Diana is always hungry. She's about 5'4", 120 pounds, with the figure of a gazelle but eats like a horse. A mystery. Ask Diana what time it is and she'll say, "Lunch time!"

Diana works with her good friend Cherri. I see both often and on occasion pick up and deliver a bag of Krystals to them, especially on rainy days. You know how girls are. Got to protect those hairdos.

Diana's a Krystals freak. Should the Krystal Corporation ever need a living testimonial to its product, it should contact Diana.

It was raining last Thursday, so I made the Krystal run.

"How many would you like?" I asked the girls.

"How many do you want, Cherri?" Diana asked her co-worker.

"Two," Cherri said.

"OK, bring us ten—and two orders of fries," Diana said.

I arrived back in their office at 11:30 A.M. with the Krystals—two for Cherri and eight for Diana—along with the fries. They were devoured immediately.

I left, but was back in the office at 12:15 P.M. I spoke to Cherri but didn't see Diana at her desk, just eight empty Krystal containers and a ripped french fries bag.

"Where's Diana?" I asked.

Cherri never looked up, but said matter-of-factly, "She's gone to lunch."

THOUGHTS ON "WORD STUFF," PONDERING

My good friend and pen pal Henry Bowden continues to write interesting sidelights in his law office in Atlanta. He is thoughtful enough to share most of them with me. I receive an envelope filled with his thoughts on various subjects about once a month, and it is always welcome. Here are some of Henry Bowden's views on selected subjects that most of us have thought about but never reduced to writing:

- On Specialized Terminology. My own profession as a lawyer is about as bad about it as you can find. For instance, we as lawyers might say "inter-spousal osculation" when non-lawyers would simply describe it as a husband and wife kissing. A doctor might well say that he had "excised the lesion," but the rest of us would say he had cut off the hickey. A real estate person would describe it by saying "the transaction was consummated," but you and I would say the house was sold. A preacher might say "the twain joined hand and hearts together as one and strove therafter mightily." But the rest of us would say "So they got married and lived happily ever after."
- On Word Stuff. I became interested recently in the expression "used to." It is really unique for it has so many different and yet clear meanings. If you formerly played golf, for instance, and you quit you might say, "I used to play golf." In that sense the phrase is substituted for the word *formerly*. On the other hand, when we change over from standard time to daylight savings time you hear lots of folks say, "I find it hard getting used to the new time." In that case it doesn't mean "formerly" but means "accustomed to." Still in explaining to the uninitiated the different clubs you would say, "Now this club is used to putt with on the putting surface." In that case the two words mean "to employ or work with" in getting something done. Talk about the Chinese language being a mystery. It seems to me from such as this that they don't have a corner on

the market. We've got our share too.

● *On Pondering.* I have known lots of folks named Ponder, but what I am talking about here is the verb "to ponder." I guess it has been occasioned by use of the word *ponder* in the Christmas story in the Bible: "and Mary pondered these things in her heart." Now then, pondering is greatly different from reminiscing. It takes two to reminisce. You get together with some other person and talk about old times. That is reminiscing. But one ponders alone and to himself. You mentally recall such things as when you first went to school, your early athletic ambitions, the first time you kissed your girl, your high school graduation, your first job and how scared you were. Your close friends and what they have meant to you in your life. Your marriage and the coming of your firstborn. The wars and your participation. Illness and recoveries. There are of course hundreds of topics; this is a good sampling. Just to sit and review some of them mentally, sometimes with regret and sometimes with a bit of pride and satisfaction. Bring them to mind, dismiss them, and go on. This is what pondering means to me. I like it because I don't ponder the unpleasant. It is great fun to ponder. I believe I will do more of it.

On Subtle Differences in Men and Women. Have you ever noticed that if you ask a lady to look at her fingernails, she will almost invariably turn her palms away from her, extend all five fingers, and look at the nails with the fingers extended? But usually when you ask a man to look at his fingernails, he will turn his palms toward himself, curl his fingers over, and look at his nails in that fashion.

THE PROPER DRESS CODE FOR THE MALL

One thing I noticed while in the Dublin Mall last Christmas was that women mostly dress alike to go mall shopping. The uniform of the day for them was what we used to call a sweat suit. I think now they are called leisure or jogging suits.

Some were dressed out in sweatshirts and jeans, but not just any old sweatshirt. If it wasn't white and decorated with holly leaves, a Christmas tree, or a hand-painted picture of Santa Claus, forget it. And whatever happened to small, medium, and large? Obviously these are on the endangered species list, having been replaced by extra-large. I saw girls not four feet tall and weighing less than ninety pounds wearing extra-large sweatshirts. Like an umbrella, I guess, they cover everything but touch nothing.

The Difference Between Misfortune and Disaster

Two philosophers were sitting at a restaurant, discussing whether there was a difference between misfortune and disaster.

"There is most certainly a difference," said one. "If the cook suddenly died and we couldn't have our dinner, that would certainly be a misfortune—but not a disaster. On the other hand, if a cruise ship carrying the Congress on a junket to the Bahamas were to sink in the middle of the ocean, that would be a disaster—but by no stretch of the imagination would it be a misfortune."

For the Good Times

I was having coffee with two good friends recently who, due to the nature of their business, are required to spend a lot of nights away from home. Both are married so the conversation drifted to whether their wives questioned their away-from-home activities when they returned.

"Mine never says a word," one, whom I'll just call Joe, said.

"I guess she just trusts me implicitly."

I then posed the question to the other, whom I'll just call Don, who replied, "Heck, mine doesn't care where I go or what I do—just as long as I don't have any fun."

Spitting and Scratching

Some time ago I had as guests on my Monday night television show three former minor league baseball players, Don Vaughn, Woody Sullivan, and Allen Thomas, who now live in Dublin. We talked for an hour about baseball as it was played in the minor leagues.

The word came to me the next day from a friend, Joe Durant, that yet another friend, Pete Raymer, had watched the show and made this observation:

"I really enjoyed the show, but it was somewhat lacking in authenticity. There was an obvious absence of spitting and scratching."

Pete's point is well taken.

A No-Win Psychiatric Situation

Natalie was the receptionist in a psychiatrist's office and obviously was very frustrated.

"I'm going to quit my job," Natalie said to her girlfriend over lunch.

"But I thought you always wanted to work for a psychiatrist," her friend said.

"He says I have an anxiety complex. When I'm late, he tells me I'm being hostile and rebellious. And when I'm on time he says I'm being compulsive."

Decisions, Decisions

The obviously expectant mother sat down in the dentist's chair and grew pale.

"What's wrong?" asked the dentist.

"I honestly don't know what's worse," she said, "having my teeth drilled or having a baby."

"Well," he said as he stood back, "make up your mind so I'll know which way to tilt the chair."

WISDOM FROM SOUTH GEORGIA

The well never seems to run dry when it comes to xeroxed tidbits of humor and wisdom. Friends supply me with them.

The latest envelope, containing several, came last week from Adel. Dan Cowart, Cook County probate judge, sent them to me after I'd been there to speak at the first Founder's Day banquet of the Cook County Historical Society.

Dan Cowart collects humorous articles and items. These were among the ones he sent me:

What Is an American?
- He will work hard on the farm so he can move into town where he can make more money so he can move back to the farm.
- He may not be able to fight his way out of a paper bag, but spends twenty bucks for a ringside seat so he can tell the professionals how to fight.
- He is the fellow who yells for the government to balance the budget, then uses his last dollar to make a down payment on a car.
- He whips the enemy, then gives him the shirt off his back and tons of money to help him get back on his feet.
- He yells for speed laws that will curtail fast driving, but won't drive a car if it can't go one hundred miles per hour.
- He knows the line-up of every baseball team in the American and National leagues, but doesn't know half the words to "The Star-Spangled Banner."
- He'll spend half a day looking for vitamin pills to make him live longer, then drive ninety miles per hour on slick pavement to make up for lost time.
- He ties up his dog but lets his sixteen-year-old, wild-as-a-tiger son go whenever he pleases.
- He is proud of his backyard, the manicured lawn and

beautiful flowers, but builds a high fence around it to keep others from seeing it.

● America has more food than any other country in the world and more diets to prevent its people from eating it.

● He will work hard and save to build an expensive house, then go on vacation and sleep in a tent in the mountains.

● Americans are the people whose eyes moisten when Old Glory passes in a parade, but just try and find a man who'll admit it.

A Short Prayer for the Workplace

Dear God, I love this place! But please be patient with me. I only work here because I am too old for a paper route, too young for Social Security, and too tired to have an affair. Amen.

A Senior Citizen's Prayer

Lord, Thou knowest I have grown old. Keep me from getting talkative on every subject and on every occasion or trying to straighten out everybody's affairs. Spare my mind from the recital of endless details, but give me the wings to get to the point. Teach me the glorious lesson that occasionally I may be mistaken. Make me thoughtful, but not moody; helpful, but not bossy. Keep me reasonably sweet, but not a saint. Some of them are hard to live with, but a sour old woman is worse. With my vast store of wisdom, it seems such a pity not to use it all; but Thou knowest, Lord, that I do want a few friends at the end. Amen.

PARADISE ON THE FLORIDA COAST

Destin, Florida, may be the best-kept secret since the Oak Ridge, Tennessee, atomic bomb project fifty years ago. No, check that: *was* the best-kept secret until the word got out a few years ago regarding its beautiful white beaches and sky-blue waters.

I first came to Destin in the mid-seventies to visit my son, Joe, who had the wisdom to come here for his first job, managing a tennis and health club, after finishing college. (Actually, Joe was in Fort Walton Beach, eight miles away.) After an absence of seventeen years I returned to Destin recently. The beaches are still white and the water still sky blue, both trademarks of this resort area on the Gulf of Mexico.

My daughter, Lisa, found it and spent her honeymoon here. She's convinced that if you live a good life, abide by the Golden Rule, and eat your vegetables, you will go to Destin when you die.

I think maybe Destin is where God spent His seventh day. The book of Genesis doesn't say so, but it doesn't say he didn't, either. Genesis 2:2 merely says that "on the seventh day God ended His work which He had made; and he rested on the seventh day from all His work which He had made."

God, in all His wisdom, could easily have chosen Destin to catch His breath after creating the heaven and the earth in just six days, a phenomenal feat when considered. But we must remember that there were no labor unions, government regulations, or environmentalists back then; and the ACLU, minimum wage, and the Supreme Court were nothing more than minuscule dots on the newly created horizon.

Destin, while still the most beautiful beach area I visit, has changed. Once the secret of its beauty was revealed to the city dwellers north of Richmond there was no stopping the influx of snowbirds from New York, New Jersey, Michigan, and the like.

The Word Spreads

Tony and Maria, natives of Brooklyn, went on vacation fifteen years ago intent on driving to Vermont. But Tony took a wrong turn just south of Peterboro, New Jersey, on U.S. 4, and ended up on Highway 98 just west of Panama City. He kept driving, ending up in Destin; and they spent two wonderful weeks there.

Once back in Brooklyn, Tony and Maria spread the news. Tony told Angelo, a fellow dock worker, about it, while Maria was singing the praises of Destin to Rosa at the deli.

Angelo told Mario about it at a bar in Newark, and Mario spilled the beans to Nunzio who drives a bread truck in Jersey City and has a brother, Carmine, in Flint, Michigan. Naturally, Nunzio told Carmine about Destin. Meanwhile, Rosa told a cousin, Carmella, who lives in Harrisburg, Pennsylvania, about it.

From there the word about Destin spread throughout the East like kudzu. And they all went, returning home to spread the word further. Within months the easterners migrated south to Destin like snowbirds, and high-rises came along with traffic jams and northern newspapers.

Sleepy Destin was awakened by what seemed like a jailbreak with horns blowing, tires screeching, and jamboxes blaring. It hasn't been back to sleep since.

I relaxed for a week on Destin's beautiful beaches, ate in its fine restaurants, and talked to some of its natives.

I concluded that a love/hate relationship exists between the locals and the snowbirds. The locals love the northern money, but would just as soon they mail it in.

PART TWO

LIFE NEVER CEASES TO AMAZE ME

The longer I live, the longer I want to live. I think that's only natural. It's like the old Chinese proverb that says, "No man grows so old but that he is convinced he will live one more year."

Due to the extension of life expectancy in this century, people are living longer. So it follows that the longer we live, the more we will experience and the more we will be amazed.

I'm amazed every day by what has been done in the way of space exploration, with astronauts now doing what I read about as fantasy as a boy in the late twenties and thirties. Back then, only Buck Rogers was flying around between planets and shooting ray guns.

I'm also amazed by what has been done in the field of medical research, organ transplants, by-passes, and plastic surgery. In my youth the major treatment came from my grandmother, medication from a great big jar of salve that was used to treat everything from sore eyes to rheumatism. My grandmother could, in all probability, take a jar of that salve today and send 90 percent of the hospital patients home within twenty-four hours. But there was no Medicare back in her day.

Surgery? My grandfather took care of that with his pocket knife. He removed splinters from fingers and toes, lanced boils, and punctured cysts—after striking a kitchen match on the seat of his pants and "sterilizing" his knife blade with it.

I am amazed at where television has gone—from nowhere to nothing. People are doing and saying things on television today that would have gotten them convicted and sent to prison forty years ago. And television advertising is aimed at the kindergarten level, and below.

A few other things that amaze me today are: shopping, fashions, vending machines, football dancing, and the sports card craze. I write about all these, and more, in this section.

Know what else? Health care costs. Good Lord! It now costs less to get sick and die than to get treated and live!

WHATEVER HAPPENED TO TRUTH IN ADVERTISING?

The more I watch television, the more I don't understand the commercials. Whatever happened to truth in advertising? The truth is, television commercials simply do not tell it like it is. Inasmuch as television has taken over the world, I think the industry should tell its viewers the truth.

Here are a few things I'd like to see in television commercials:

• I'd like to hear a guy in a beer commercial burp now and then and excuse himself after a dozen or so to go to the rest room. Seems to me that both are normal reactions for beer drinkers.

• I'd like to see the dog in the Alpo commercial turn up his nose at the bowl of dog food and then sit there and scratch under his flea collar.

• I'd like to see the man advertising Roach Prufe stop in the middle of the commercial long enough to stomp a pair of roaches with the sole of his shoe, the only sure-fire way to get rid of the little devils.

• I want to see the girl who takes the Honda out for a test drive ride all over Atlanta looking for a parking place like I have to do. What does she do? She pulls into a wide open space right in front of the Ritz-Carlton, smack-dab in the middle of downtown at 4:45 P.M.

Those are but a few. I have more. One of my favorites is a thing called Trim-Trak, a little contraption that resembles a railroad motorcar and slides back and forth on a little piece of railroad track. A long, lean, and lanky girl who looks like Twiggy's sister makes the thing move back and forth by pulling on a handle. The TV pitch is that Trim-Trak will slim a person down and transform the body from the Roseanne Arnold look to that of a figure skater.

Well, the girl operating the Trim-Trak on television doesn't need it. If the Trim-Trak people want to show it like it is, why don't they put some ole gal on the thing who's shaped like a Dempsey dumpster and has arms like Popeye? And show her huffin', puffin', and sweatin' a lot. The model who demonstrates the Trim-Trak on television doesn't sweat at all. In fact, she ain't even breathin' hard when she stops pumpin' and slides the machine underneath the sofa.

Also, I have no reason to doubt the mechanical qualifications of Mr. Goodwrench. But why not smear a little grease on his cheek, forehead, and one ear? And dirty his hands and fingernails up a little bit, and put a dab or two of used motor oil on the shoulder and back of his shirt as evidence that he did indeed crawl up under at least one car to check the oil pan, differential, and transmission. Turn off the microphone but move in close with the camera in order to capture his expression when the vice-grip pliers slip off a bolt holding the alternator brace, causing him to scrape the knuckles of his right hand on the fan. Also show the anxiety on his face when he tries desperately to replace a stubborn nut in a remote area underneath the power steering unit. Watch him fume as the overheated radiator spews boiling water all over him like Mount Vesuvius at the height of an eruption. To me, this would make a Mr. Goodwrench commercial much more believable.

Finally, there's the shampoo commercial that shows a fella with all the shampoo sittin' on top of his head. Friends, that just ain't the way it happens. What about the eyes? I ain't believin' the shampoo commercial 'til it shows me a guy who's blind as a bat with shampoo in both eyes desperately trying to feel his way to the towel holder in search of relief. And show him running into the commode and lavatory. Show him stumbling over the trash can and stumping his toe on an open closet door.

SHOPPING TODAY IS AN ADVENTURE

I am not a good shopper. I'm also not a thrifty shopper, much to my chagrin. I don't look for sales. I'm old enough to remember when stores had but two sales a year. Today, stores have sales every week.

I was in Nashville, Tennessee, last Friday and Saturday to attend a few functions associated with the release of my book, *Why the South Lost the War/And Other Things I Don't Understand.* As I was getting dressed Friday evening, I discovered that I hadn't packed any socks and had to be at a reception in half an hour. I didn't panic. I concluded that I would stop in at the first clothing store I saw on the way and buy a pair.

I spotted one in a quaint little suburban shopping center, appropriately named the Gent's Shoppe. Caution: Be alert for cute little suburban shopping centers with *shoppes.* I walked into the Gent's Shoppe and was immediately approached by a very well-dressed, well-groomed, and generally neat young lady.

"May I help you, sir?" she asked politely.

"Yes, thank you," I said. "I need a pair of navy blue, over-the-calf socks."

"All right," she said and walked a few steps to a sock bin. She returned with the socks. She said they were navy blue. I wouldn't know. They could have been orange or yellow. I am very color blind.

She dropped the socks in a quaint little bag with a picture of either a king or a prince on it. I didn't ask which.

"Will there be anything else?" she asked.

"No, thank you," I replied.

"All right, that will be $13.84 with tax," she said with a straight face.

"Uh, ma'am . . . I only wanted one pair," I said.

"Right, one pair," she said.

I almost dropped my dentures. Heck, my shoes didn't cost

much more than that. But I took the socks, watched my twenty disappear somewhere into the far reaches of the cash register, and received $6.16 change.

I took the socks for two reasons: (1) I failed, as usual, to ask the price at the outset; (2) I didn't have time to hunt for another store.

I couldn't resist asking one question. "These socks ain't by chance on sale, are they?"

"No, sir! Never! Those socks are prime merchandise," she said.

"I'm glad to know that," I said.

Everything went well, but nobody commented on my socks. There I was, a millionaire from the calf down and nobody said a word.

I can hardly wait for another function worthy of my $13.84, navy blue, over-the-calf socks. I'll just remove them from my safety deposit box and wear those suckers.

One of my favorite stories about sales concerns two merchants, one from Pennsylvania and one from New York. They were vacationing at Miami Beach when they met and this conversation ensued:

"Hello, John."

"Hello, Michael."

"How's business?" John asked.

"Great! Just great!" said Michael. "We had a $300,000 fire in January and a $200,000 flood in April."

"You did?" asked a wide-eyed John.

"Yep," said Michael. "How's it going with you?"

"We had a small fire just after Christmas and made a little over $90,000," John replied somberly.

"Well, I have to be going," Michael said, and walked away.

Michael hadn't gone fifty feet when he heard John yelling to him, "Michael! Wait up!"

Michael stopped and waited. John arrived almost out of breath.

"Tell me something," John puffed.

"What is it?"

"How do you start a flood?"

MONDAY IS THE WEEK'S WORST

Most people will agree that February is the worst month of the year. Nothing happens in February other than Valentine's Day when wives and sweethearts receive candy and flowers and the florists and candy shops mop up. It's not so important what is sent to a wife or sweetheart; but it is very important that something be sent. Otherwise, the St. Valentine's Day Massacre may happen all over again. Pay absolutely no attention if the little woman says, "Don't get me anything for Valentine's Day this year." Believe me, she doesn't mean a word of it.

OK, so much for the drab month of February. What's the worst day of the week? No contest. It's Monday, of course.

What could be worse than having to crawl out of a nice warm bed on a rainy Monday morning after having had an award-winning weekend and facing the fact that you must go to work? Even people who don't have jobs hate to get up and go looking for work on Mondays or dragging down to the unemployment office to exchange tales with fellow out-of-workers about the great jobs that got away.

I suggested several years ago that payday should be changed from Friday to Monday. That way, Monday becomes a favorite day rather than the black sheep of the work week. Besides, if payday were changed from Friday to Monday, there's no way the paycheck could be blown over a weekend.

There was a calendar on the market a few years back (1982) called "The Monday Haters Calendar." I received one from a friend at Christmas 1981. I blew 1982, but kept the now out-of-date calendar.

The calendar's publishers researched examples of noted snafus that happened on Monday:

- Napoleon invaded Russia on a Monday.

- The *Titanic* sank on a Monday.

• Patty Hearst was kidnapped on a Monday.

• The nation's worst air disaster happened on Monday in Chicago when an American Airlines DC-10 crashed May 25, 1979, and 273 people were killed.

"America may love baseball, hot dogs, apple pie, and Japanese cars," says the calendar's promotion man, Ron Kalb, "but it hates Mondays."

Here are a few that didn't make the calendar:

• What day of the week is traffic worst? Monday.

• It seems that school book reports are always due on Monday and ruin a weekend. Ditto with report cards.

• If Ma Bell cuts off your telephone, more than likely it will happen on a Monday.

• Your favorite restaurant is closed on Monday.

• Howard Cosell was on "Monday Night Football" for—how long? Three hundred years?

• Monday is the day everyone begins a diet. The following Monday is when most say, "Awwww! To heck with it!"

• The office coffee machine always breaks on Monday following a rip-roaring weekend.

• Pro football rookies hate Mondays. That's the day of the week the Turk shows up to tell 'em they're cut.

• I think most dentists do root canals on Mondays.

• No one I know gets paid on Monday.

• The mailbox is usually filled with junk mail and bills on Mondays.

• Most wives hate Monday nights during football season because that's the night they become TV widows.

• Monday is the day you face all the work in the office that you failed to do the previous Friday.

All my life I've heard people say, "Where have you been? I haven't seen you in a month of Sundays." I have never heard anybody make reference to a "month of Mondays," but I think it would be longer.

QUESTIONS! QUESTIONS! VERY IRRITATING!

"To be, or not to be; that is the question." I'm not even sure that's a question, but if so it is by no means *the* question but *a* question.

I put my brain in gear recently and jotted down some questions—questions that, in my estimation, are irritating. You've probably heard some, if not all, of them. Take a look and determine for yourself if you consider any or all of these questions irritating, or if they produce the urge to kill:

- At the fast food drive-through: "Want fries with that?"
- At the convenience store checkout: "Izzatit?"
- At the cash register of the all-night coffee shop: "Don't you have anything smaller than a twenty?"
- At the corporate office the telephone receptionist asks, "He's away from his desk right now. Can I tell him who's calling, and what it's about?"
- At the hospital admitting office: "Do you have a supplemental policy, or is this it?"
- On the telephone just as you sit down for dinner: "May I talk with you for a while about a great new stock offering?"
- At the bridge club: "You mean you don't have a VCR?"
- At the hairdresser: "Did I hear you say your daughter is getting married . . . again?"
- At dinner: "Dad, can I have $75 to buy two tickets to the Grateful Dead concert Saturday night?"
- At dinner: "Wasn't today report card day, son?"
- At or near the Forsyth exit on I-16: "May I see your driver's license and insurance card?"
- At bedtime: "Daddy, can I get two hamsters?"
- At work: "Do you have any idea what time we begin work in this office?"
- At the restaurant: "Can I substitute sliced tomatoes for the cauliflower, pole beans for the beets, and get an extra order of black-eyed peas instead of the collards?"
- At the dress shop: "You

didn't *really* think you could get into a size six, did you?"

• At the salad bar: "Do you really intend to eat all that?"

• At a dinner party: "You don't mind if I smoke, do you?"

• At school: "You're not serious about going to the Junior-Senior Prom with *him*, are you?"

• At home, just the two of you: "Whadda ya mean you're gonna buy a bikini to wear to th' beach this summer? You *are* joking, right?"

• At the office, on the telephone: "Have you mailed my alimony check yet?"

• At home on Saturday morning: "Are you going to paint the kitchen and clean out the garage today, or do you plan to play golf again?"

• At a cocktail party: "Is that your natural hair color?"

• At the mall parking lot (six weeks after the birth of your baby): "When are you going to have your baby?"

• At home, getting ready to go to work: "Hey! Are you gonna stay in the bathroom all morning?"

• At the café: "You got plans when you get off tonight, baby?"

• At home, during Saturday morning breakfast: "Would you like to go shopping with me this afternoon, dear?"

• At the stadium: "Will the owner of the 1989 Buick Riviera with license number GTL-566 that is parked in a handicapped zone and blocking the ramp please move it?"

• At a class reunion: "You mean you *really* did get married?"

• At the ice cream section of the supermarket: "You mean you're *not* on a diet?"

• Sitting across from the boss: "And just what makes you think you deserve a raise?"

• At a government office: "Did you bring all the forms?"

• On the golf course: "Was that your son I saw at the mall yesterday wearing an earring?"

• At home: "Son, does that infernal noise box in your room have a volume control knob on it?"

• On the telephone, returning an "urgent" call: "I'm sorry, he's very busy right now. Would you like me to put you on hold?"

HURRICANE YULETIDE

One Saturday night last December I did a dumb thing. I drove right into the eye of Hurricane Yuletide that hit the Macon Mall with a vengeance about 2:00 P.M. that sent women and children scurrying madly from store to store while men sat and watched. And I reminded myself repeatedly, "Bo, you're smarter than this."

I witnessed a killer typhoon while aboard a hospital ship docked at Okinawa in September 1945. It was nothing more than a summer breeze compared to the hurricane at Macon Mall.

I spent four hours right in the middle of Hurricane Yuletide, three of them in the recovery room at Ruby Tuesday's. And that's *all* I spent, with the exception of the unbelievable price for a single dip of vanilla ice cream: $1.78. Recession? What recession? Back when I first started buying single dips of vanilla ice cream for a nickel, you could have made a down payment on a dairy for $1.78. The price of ice cream has gone crazy. I gagged on every lick.

Finished with my ice cream, I walked into a fashionable department store. I looked at what I considered to be a regular, run-of-the-mill sport shirt. It had some fella's name on it just above the left pocket. I thought perhaps my oldest grandson would like it. I fingered the price tag—$95! I almost suffered a repeat of my 1981 heart attack. Heck, that's twice as much as I paid for my first suit.

I walked outside and sat down on one of the mall benches to recover from the shock. You're familiar with the benches, I'm sure. They're harder and colder than an X-ray table and constructed to resemble same. The mall folks don't want you sittin'. They want you up, walkin', and shoppin'. And if you suddenly suffer an acute attack of spendinitis, there are surgeons masquerading as store clerks and cashiers to take care of you. They can make an incision in your wallet, remove a benign fifty-dollar bill, and suture the wallet back up before you can say, "How much did you say that was?"

While in the recovery room at Ruby Tuesday's, I reflected on the hour I'd spent upstairs braving Hurricane Yuletide. I reached certain conclusions, like these:

- Christmas shopping in malls is for women. They love it. The rougher it gets the better they like it.
- Men are dragged along for three reasons: (1) To provide cash in the event their women either run out of checks or wear the numbers off their credit cards; (2) To lug the heavy packages to the car; (3) To sit on X-ray tables and remain available in case of a cash emergency.
- Nobody vacates a parking space once they are lucky enough to find one. And at the end of the shopping day there are usually more shopping carts than cars in the parking lot.
- Mall shopping hours? Hah! If the stores remained open until 4:00 A.M. the women would still be shop-hopping, and the men would still be sitting on the X-ray tables.
- Nobody ever gets through Christmas shopping. There's always *one more* gift to buy.
- Ralph Lauren and Tommy Hilfiger have taken over the men's shops.
- No matter how much merchandise is purchased, Macy's, Belk's, Penney's, Wal-Mart, and K-Mart seem to have just as much stuff in them when they close at night as when they opened in the morning.
- *Every* store has a sale going on, every day.
- Only women buy *anything* that has to be assembled. Men shy away from them like the plague. And there's always a screw, nut, or bolt missing. The directions? Obviously written by a sadist or an engineering dropout.
- In some of the stores you have to wait on yourself, while in others they hire salespeople to ignore you.
- When the store is out of it, you'll have a coupon for it; but when you don't have a coupon for it, the store has plenty of it.
- Finally, if you're suffering from an acute case of spendinitis, have faith. Recovery usually comes in late January or early February when the credit card bills have been paid for.

THE HEIGHT OF FRUSTRATION

I've heard the expression "the height of frustration" all my life. But what is the height of frustration? I'm not sure I know, but I think it varies depending on the individual.

I can think of many experiences, mostly little aggravating things, that when they happened I was sure it was the height of frustration. Here are a few that you may be able to relate to:

• You arrive at the supermarket checkout, your shopping cart filled to overflowing. The cashier enters each item in the cash register and, after the final item has been entered, she renders her verdict: "That comes to $63.87," she says.

And there you stand with $59.12, no checkbook, no food stamps, and six impatient shoppers in line behind you chomping at the bit.

• You're getting dressed to go to a formal party, the social event of the year. You can't find your cuff links. In an unusual twist, your wife is ready and waiting, but no matter how hard you search, no cuff links.

• The bus to the big game will leave in fifteen minutes, with or without you. You're dressed out in your Bulldog pants, Bulldog shirt, Bulldog cap, and have an ample supply of Alpo in your tote bag. But you can't find your ticket. You search and disrupt desk drawers, shirt pockets, the glove compartment, over the sun visor, in the trunk, on and inside the refrigerator, and in all the trash cans. No ticket. You harbor a strong desire to blame somebody, but can't. You live alone.

• You have less than fifteen minutes to finish dressing and get to the church for the wedding. The bride is the daughter of your best friend. You tie the shoestring of your left shoe. Next, the shoestring to your right one. The shoestring breaks, the one you've been promising yourself you'd replace every day for weeks.

● You drive 176 miles, from Lake Sinclair to Waycross, to see your daughter play basketball. But upon arrival you learn that the game isn't being played in Waycross, but Stillmore. It starts in fifteen minutes, and you're two hours away.

● You are five minutes away from speaking to 250 members of a ladies' club in Valdosta, and your zipper gets stuck—in the down position.

● You are driving along after midnight on I-16 between Metter and Soperton, heading home from Savannah. It's cold. You are tired and sleepy. Your left rear tire expires, and every breath of air exits through a nail hole. You raise the trunk lid, remove the spare tire. Then, you reach for the jack. No jack! And five hundred cars pass you by.

No choice. You drive to Dublin, at three miles per hour, ruining the left rear tire and waking everybody on Academy Avenue. You arrive at Brinson's Chevron Service Center at 3:15 A.M. Your left rear tire looks like a pit bulldog got hold of it. You park your three-legged car, leave a hastily written note for Big Dave underneath the windshield wiper, and walk home in the cold.

● You're almost finished writing your Monday column on a rainy and stormy Sunday night. You finger the computer for that finishing touch only to hear a loud clap of thunder (is there any such thing as a quiet clap of thunder?), lightning cracks, and everything on your computer screen disappears to wherever computer characters disappear to following a crack of lightning. What you're thinking can't be put in a newspaper column, and there's nothing to do but start over and hope and pray the lightning holds off for a few minutes.

VENDING MACHINE FRUSTRATION

For years I've been fighting vending machines that refuse to do what they're supposed to do. Half the time they don't work, and when they do they don't deliver what I paid for.

Here's what happens to me. I insert my coins and pull the lever for a candy bar and get cheese crackers. I pull the lever for chewing gum and get potato chips or pork skins. More often than not I drop four dimes and a nickel in the slot, pull the lever designated for a Hershey bar, and nothing happens. I jiggle the coin return thingamajig and get back two dimes and a nickel. The other two dimes? Where they go I'll never know. And just try and find somebody who will take the responsibility for the foul-up and see what happens.

"We don't know nothing about it," says the girl behind the counter. "We just lease the space to the vending company. You'll have to speak to the manager, Mr. Johnson, about it."

"Fine. Would you tell Mr. Johnson I'd like to speak to him?"

"Can't. He's on a cruise and won't be back for three weeks."

You stand the same chance of getting your money back from Johnson as you would from a television evangelist or a flim-flam artist.

Here's another thing that prompts an urge to go on a break-and-destroy mission: After depositing my coins and pulling the lever for the item I want, always up top, it falls off the Empire State Building and gets caught in a mass of twisted wire about the eighth floor or ends up crossways at the exit chute. No matter how much shaking and kicking I do, it won't budge, and a hand won't go up into the chute far enough to grab it. Trust me. I know this to be a fact.

Coin-operated vending machines offer an endless variety of items, from stamps to nail clippers, soft drinks to peanuts, cigarettes to self-portraits, combs and newspapers.

Ahhhhh . . . newspapers. Not only do the darn machines play tricks, but some of the folks who fill them are a day or two late now and then, the large dailies I'm talking about. This happens to me with alarming regularity, especially late at night when I really want a newspaper before retiring.

What happens is this: I approach the newspaper machine in pitch-black darkness. I insert my coins, remove a newspaper, and drive home where I settle down in my favorite chair with a reading lamp over my shoulder. Somewhere along about page seven, section C, what I'm reading has a familiar ring to it, and well it should. There I sit on a Thursday night reading the same newspaper I bought and read on Monday! There's nothing more aggravating to a newspaper addict than to deposit money in the machine and end up reading Monday's paper on Thursday.

Now, a word about coin-operated coffee machines. I'm convinced they're programmed at the factory to tilt the cup at forty-five degrees when it falls into place. What happens is you put your forty cents in the slot, select the desired combination of cream and sugar—black, black with sugar, extra sugar, cream, extra cream, and so on—and then stand back and watch. The little cup, about the size of a thimble, falls from outer space and sits sideways at the pre-programmed forty-five-degree angle. Then, half your coffee goes into the cup and the other half disappears down a drainage system installed for just such an occasion.

OK, try to slide the glass covering up and remove the half-thimble full of coffee at the same time. Two will get you one that the hot stuff will saturate your wristwatch or shoes should you succeed in removing it from the machine.

I've been fighting coin-operated vending machines, and losing. I think I know why. The darn things are made by the government.

HEALTH CARE COSTS AREN'T FUNNY, BUT THEY'RE A JOKE

I don't understand what's happened to health care costs. In the 1950s a woman, usually married, could have a baby for about $300. Today? Between $4,000 and $5,000. Why?

Are 1990s babies more streamlined than 1950s babies? Do they arrive with more options? Aren't the features and fixtures the same?

Here are a few deserved jabs at the medical profession and the high cost of the services it offers:

- It now costs more to go to the hospital than it used to cost to go to medical school.

- Private hospitals have strange ways of making money. I know one that sells tickets for visiting hours.

- Fella said he was operated on at a great hospital— Our Lady of Malpractice. "Five years ago they spent $3 million on a recovery room, and it hasn't been used yet."

- Today's hospitals don't kid around. I won't say what happens if you don't pay your bill, but did you ever have kidney stones put back in?

- A hospital's a place that keeps you three days if you have big troubles, three months if you have big insurance.

- Last week I only ate one-hundred-dollars-a-plate dinners: I was in the hospital.

- Yesterday I had my first bath in bed in the hospital. A nurse washed me down, then gave me a wet cloth and said, "You know what to do with this." I didn't really, but now I have the cleanest windows on the fourth floor.

- It must be wonderful to be a doctor. In what other job could you ask a girl to take her clothes off, look her over at your leisure, and then send a bill to her husband?

- The phone rang and the doctor answered. "Hello . . .

this is who? . . . Dolly Parton? . . . You say you sprained your big toe? . . . Stay right where you are. I'll get my stethoscope and be right over!"

• The nurses always say, "How's our leg today?" or "How's our back today?" But when I touched our thigh, she slapped our face.

• The little guy stood at the prescription counter eyeing his medicine bottle containing very expensive pills.

"Anything wrong?" asked the druggist.

"Well, uh, this label says 'Take until gone' and I was just wondering . . . does that mean the medicine, my money, or me?"

• Then there's the M.D. who got a call from a very excited woman: "Doctor! Doctor! My poodle just swallowed thirty Bufferins! What should I do?"

"Give him a headache, what else?" said the doctor.

• It's a fact: Last year, Americans spent more than $18 billion on medical care. It's really doing the job. More and more doctors are getting well.

• My doctor has a great stress test. It's called "the bill."

• I was practically cured of back pains by acupuncture when I called my doctor and told him that the pains had returned. He yawned and said, "Just take two thumb tacks and call me in the morning."

• Overheard at the bridge club: "My operation was so serious that when the surgeon finished operating they put me in the expensive care unit."

• The best way to tell real doctors from imposters is the way they hold their medical instruments. A fake doctor doesn't know the proper way to grip a putter.

• "I'm going to operate on Mrs. Green," the doctor told the intern.

"Oh? What does she have?"

"Ten thousand dollars."

• The credo of the men of medicine: "Always write your prescriptions illegibly and your bills plainly."

• I know a young doctor fresh out of medical school. I don't think he's making very much money yet because his stethoscope is on a party line.

THE RIDICULOUS COSTS OF HEALTH CARE

I don't think I've ever heard as much talk about the high cost of health care as I did in our recent presidential campaign. All candidates had "the answer." "Runaway costs," one said. "Spiraling health insurance premiums," echoed another. "Drastic situation," called out the third.

Each had a solution. They promised the moon. By mid-October I wouldn't have been surprised if they'd promised to put a doctor in every den, a nurse in every bedroom, a clinic in every basement, an ambulance in every garage, and a 911 cellular phone in every car.

The advent of Medicare and Medicaid on July 1, 1966, made health care folks rich(er). Any doctor or druggist who isn't walking in high cotton these days just ain't trying. Even some of the prescription dispensers who could hardly make it prior to July 1, 1966, inherited a windfall.

They see about fifty patients a day complaining of everything from gout to rheumatism, reach for the old prescription pad, scribble on it, and stick the patient, the government, or some insurance company $40 for a five-minute office visit. That comes to $480 an hour/$3,600 a day.

The sad commentary is that about 90 percent of the patients would have gotten well on their own anyway.

• Here's a true story: A very nice Dublin lady, highly respected, visited her doctor about ten years ago. She received the usual prescription, a $30 bill for her five minutes with her doctor, and an appointment to return in thirty days.

Later, the lady went to the hospital to visit a good friend. While there the doctor came in—the same doctor she had used for years. He spent a few seconds at the bedside of her friend and, as he was leaving, said, "And how are you feeling, Sarah?" (not her true name).

"Very well," she said.

Can you believe this? In a few days Sarah received a bill from the doctor for his "hospital" visit—$18.

When Sarah finished telling me this story, I asked her what she did about the bill.

"I didn't pay it!" she said. "And what's more, I called him up and blessed him out!"

• Here's another one: Two years ago I went into Same Day Surgery for arthroscopic surgery on my right knee—torn ligaments. I went in at 9:30 A.M. and was back home at 3:30 P.M. The hospital bill? Try $2,700 and change. I was even charged $4.50 for the 59-cent Bic throwaway razor the nurse used to shave my knee—and I didn't even get the razor!

• Health care wasn't always as ridiculous as it is today. Here's proof: I had lunch not long ago at the Dexter Cafe. The owner, James L. Wood, said he had something to show me.

He showed me two handwritten bills from the Dublin Sanatorium itemizing charges for the hospitalization of his mother, Mrs. J. J. Wood, who gave birth to a baby. The bills are both dated January 17, 1920. Take a look:

Mrs. J. J. Wood.
Number of Days in The
    Hospital, (3) at $2.50 Per
    Day— $7.50
Anesthetic. $$$$$$$ 10.00
Operating Room
    Fee. $$$$$$$$$$$$$ 5.00
Medicine. $$$$$$$$$ 1.75
Special Nurse
    (Board). $$$$$$$$$ 3.00
Total. $$$$$$$$$$$$ 27.00

Baby Wood
Number of Days in
    Hospital, (2) at $2.50 per
    day— $5.00
Two Bottles 1.20
Operating Room
    Fee .... .80
Total $7.00

CAN ANYONE OUT THERE SING OUR NATIONAL ANTHEM?

I watch very little TV, but listen to a bunch of radio. That's because I spend more time in the driver's seat of my car than in my living room recliner. Basically, I listen to talk shows and Braves games.

In most cases I never hear the completion of "The Star-Spangled Banner" because of the way most singers add their own special touches to what Francis Scott Key had in mind. They go something like this:

"Ohhhhh, say can you seee-EEE, by the dawn's early li-IIIII-ght. What so-OOO pro-UUU-dly we HAIL-ed, at the twlight's laaaa-eeeeest gleaming . . ." and so on.

I don't want wrinkles in "The Star-Spangled Banner." Sing it the way it was intended to be sung.

I am not a Skip Carey fan, but to give the devil his due, he did come up with a timely comment, into a live microphone, when some woman was straining her way through the latest rendition of "The Star-Spangled Banner" before a Braves game. She rambled on and on, inserting her own wrinkles. The game could have been in the bottom of the third by the time she finally finished.

After what seemed like an eternity, the ole gal was still moaning and wrinkling. She was somewhere in the neighborhood of "o'er the land of the free" when these words by Caray came over the air, "Anybody got a gun?"

I know! You're saying that I'm belittling women. No way! The two finest renditions of "The Star-Spangled Banner" I've heard in the past forty years were performed by women— Whitney Houston for the troops in the Persian Gulf War and Miriam Moadd, who sang it before a Braves game. (Miriam is a former newsperson at WSB-Radio in Atlanta and a very talented singer.) Both sing the song wrinkle-free.

The worst rendition was by Roseanne Barr before a game in San Diego. She should have been indicted for murder, because that's what she did to "The Star-Spangled Banner": she murdered it.

I refuse to listen to the improvisers. When I hear the song, I want goosebumps to appear on my neck, cold chills to run up and down my spine, a lump to come up in my throat—and I'm not ashamed of a tear or two.

By far the best rendition by male or female I ever heard was the one on an old record by Gordon MacRae in the early fifties at the Sparta, Georgia, baseball park when Sparta was in the Georgia State League. The PA announcer must have used it before every home game for twelve years because it was scratchy. When Gordon MacRae sang it sounded like bacon frying in the background. But no matter, he sang the song right.

If the professional franchise insists on having somebody sing "The Star-Spangled Banner" before every game, they should at least line up somebody who knows how to sing it. Otherwise, put on the Elvis rendition of "Dixie." That would really put goosebumps on the back of my neck, send cold chills up and down my spine, cause a lump to come up in my throat, and probably bring a tear or two.

But that ain't gonna happen because no franchise or organization in Georgia has the guts to play it these days, not even down here in the land of cotton.

THIS IS FOOTBALL?

Football used to be fun to watch. No more. I can find better things to do than watch the gyrations, tribal dances, struts, and body contortions by players after having done what they're paid megabucks to do.

An offensive player scores, and the spasms and convulsions set in. Then the chicken walk takes over.

A defensive player makes a tackle, gets up, raises his arms to the heavens, and says, "Shower me with accolades!"

It began when coaches added offensive and defensive choreographers to their staffs. You can spot 'em if you look closely.

The head coach is easy to spot. He's the guy fitted out with more electronic equipment than an astronaut. A good shot of lightning would send him to that Great Superbowl in the sky. Another dead giveaway is the little boy who trails him, holding enough power cord to rewire ESPN.

The offensive coordinator is also easy to spot. He's the one who, when his offense has scored but a lone field goal and it's late in the fourth quarter, gives the appearance that his General Dynamics stock has dropped from $104¾ to $13⅛, his feet hurt, he's overdrawn at the bank, he's nine years shy of Social Security and Medicare, and his wife is in the stands reading a newspaper—the "Help Wanted" section of the classifieds.

The defensive coordinator is equally as easy to spot. He's the one who, after his defense has given up 52 points and it's not yet halftime, gives the appearance that his daughter ran off the night before with the defensive end's younger brother, a rock musician, and left this note: "Daddy: Don't worry. We'll be fine. Raymond says that Newark is a nice place to live and raise a family. Good luck tomorrow. Love, Sheila."

While not easy, I finally spotted the offensive and defensive choreographers. Their pants give them away.

Offensive choreographers wear ballet tights and loiter behind the cheerleaders.

Defensive choreographers wear leotards and hang out near the Gatorade barrel.

I've interviewed both.

The offensive choreographer, Pierre Rabut (pronounced Rayboo), a native of Bordeaux, France, is chief choreographer for the Atlanta Ballet Company but works with the Falcon offense during football season.

"I work exclusively with running backs, wide receivers, and ends on movements to execute in the end zone after scoring," Pierre said. "When I came on board, most couldn't put one foot in front of the other. I started with adaptations from basic ballet moves like the Pas Allé (a simple walking step), the Pas du Basque (swaying from side to side, the right leg executing a circular movement from the hip), and the Pas de Bourré (transferring the weight from one foot to the other)."

"Were they able to make the transition from the dance studio to the football field?" I asked.

"Oh, yes," Pierre said proudly. "In no time at all I upgraded them to the Pas du Chat (one foot jumps over the other, executed on the diagonal, with the feet drawn one after the other up to the knee of the opposite leg). And a wide receiver, Ryshenka Washington, took to the movements like a swan to a lake. After three weeks he was executing a perfect Ronde de Jamba (a rotary movement on the ground of the working leg, executed from the hip, outwards, when the leg is extended first to the front with the foot fully pointed and then swept round to the side and back through, foot in first, to the front again, or when executed in reverse starting from the fourth position back and sweeping round to the side and front)."

"That sounds complicated," I said.

"For some, but not for Ryshenka," Pierre allowed. "He progressed so well that he made second team All-Pro strutter with his Ronde de Jamba. It's a motivator. He told the press more than once that scoring is secondary. His jubilation comes from performing his Ronde de Jamba, and his adrenalin flows like at no other time, other than contract time of course."

"It's just ballet steps they're doing?" I asked.

"Oh, no!" Pierre squealed. "Most have developed their own end zone moves. Like Bobby Joe Braxton, a running back, and his 'Peacock Parade'; Jeremiah Armstrong, a split end, and his 'Cripple Chicken Chop.' Jeremiah is a shoo-in to make the All-

Pro Strutter's Team. And Walter Lee Witherspoon, a wide receiver, perfected his 'Vertebrae Vibrations' end zone strut after several sessions with a Marietta chiropractor."

Let's look on the other side of the line at the defensive choreographer for the New York Giants, Roberto Rouchet (pronounced "Roo-shay").

Roberto is a graduate of the London Contemporary Dance School and is chief choreographer for the New York School of Modern Dance in Greenwich Village. Saturday nights he works as a hit man for the Mafia.

His pride and joy is Anthony ("Kamikaze") Brown, a left cornerback who won the National Association of Defensive Strutter's "Twinkletoes Award" in 1990. The inscription on the plaque reads: "In recognition for having been selected the best 'After Tackle Strutter' in the NFL."

"He was a proud man as he strutted to the podium at the awards banquet with the band playing the organization's theme song, 'Darktown Strutters Ball,'" Roberto said. "I'll never forget what he said in his acceptance speech. 'I would rather win this award than the Heisman or the Super Bowl MVP trophy,' he said with tears in his eyes. There wasn't a dry eye in the place, and Kamikaze's mama was boo-hooing."

"Very impressive, Roberto," I said. "But what moves exactly do you teach your defensive players?"

"Basically head rolls, hip isolations, spine curls, contractions, back and forward kicks, body arcs, parallel jumps, side stretches, transition steps, tribal dances . . . things like that," he said. "Then, they make innovations and expand on them."

Next season should be a great one for Roberto's strutters. He has a cornerback, Gene ("Wild Man") Montgomery, who has almost perfected his "Achy Breaky Back" routine, patterned after that silly Billy Ray Cyrus song. What Wild Man does is time his hit on a wide receiver at the height of his leap to catch a pass. He then cracks him with all his might in the small of his back, intent on breaking it. Then, as the receiver writhes, twists, and squirms on the turf in obvious agony, Wild Man executes hip twists and neck isolations in the manner of Billy Ray Cyrus, making sure that the TV cameras can see his number—27—clearly.

Then there's Leroy ("Bubba") Robertson, former alligator wrestler, star performer with the Waycross Ballet Company, and offensive guard turned defensive tackle who hates quarterbacks. His specialty is infiltrating the offensive backfield, ramming a head and shoulder into the quarterback's midsection, wrapping his arms in an armlock around his body, and slamming him to the turf while grinding his head and shoulder deeper into his midsection. If the quarterback is able to get up, Bubba figures he made a bad tackle. If not, Bubba does a buck dance, lets out a Rebel yell, and struts around and over the quarterback while giving the well-known Redneck salute.

"Is there a name for Bubba's routine?" I asked.

"Yes," replied Roberto, "The Nutcracker."

This is football? Who needs it?

Not me.

THE SPORTS CARD CRAZE HAS GONE CRAZY

The world of sports memorabilia went crazy as a loon several years ago with the resurgence of baseball cards. Cards that once sold for a dime began going for forty or fifty dollars and on occasion for three or four hundred.

On the heels of the cards came baseball warm-up jackets, bats, baseballs, posters, and photographs, along with football, basketball, and hockey cards and associated items. And the players began signing autographs at card shows for twenty-five or thirty dollars. The leeches were out in force, and that closed the door on the whole scam for me.

A biggie in the memorabilia business in Tennessee publishes an annual catalog for collectors. I received one last week. How I got on their mailing list I'll never know. I made it as far as page three before turning back to the address label to verify that my name appeared there.

My first inclination was to drop the catalog in the trash can, along with Publisher's Clearing House Sweepstakes, *Reader's Digest* Sweepstakes, and several brochures featuring millions in cash and merchandise that I may have won. I didn't. I dropped it in the "hold" basket on my desk.

The catalog contains offerings that verify the insanity of the sports memorabilia world. Here are a few:

- Authentic 1951 Yankees team jacket from Mickey Mantle's rookie year: $299.
- Replica of Mickey Mantle's 1951 Louisville Slugger bat, signed by Mantle: $1,750.
- Reggie Jackson bat and baseball, signed by Jackson: $779.90.
- Signed photograph of Joe Montana: $299.95.
- Signed Magic Johnson Los Angeles Lakers jersey: $549.95.
- Magic Johnson Signed Collection: (1) an actual piece of the Forum's floor, the floor he ran on; (2) #32 Lakers game jersey; (3) of-

ficial NBA basketball; (4) 8x10 Lakers photo; (5) a signed letter to you from Magic. In a 4½' by 4½' black lacquer and plexiglass frame: $3,995.

• Dan Marino-signed Dolphin helmet: $349.95.

• Dan Marino-signed #13 Dolphin game jersey: $369.95.

• Official Spalding basketball, signed by Magic Johnson and Larry Bird: $499.95.

• Ten framed Wilt Chamberlain basketball cards: $399.95.

So much for the "inexpensive" items. Let's move on to the big stuff, like hockey.

We don't know a whole lot about the National Hockey League in the South, but apparently there are sections of the country where the sport is very popular. I recall what comedian Rodney Dangerfield had to say about the sport after attending his first game.

"How'd you like it?" a friend asked the next day.

"Know what? I went to a fight and a hockey game broke out," Dangerfield allowed.

The final two offerings in the catalog have to do with hockey, the Los Angeles Kings who feature Wayne Gretzky as their star. Take your pick, or order both.

• "Fly with the Kings." Join the Los Angeles Kings as they travel to an away game. Package for two includes round trip airfare with the team, hotel accommodations, and two tickets to the game. Only ten packages available: $5,000.

Heck, that's more than I paid for my first house!

• The Official Los Angeles Kings Boeing 727. Limited signed edition of one. The previous owner was the president of Mexico, who used the jet only occasionally for official duties. The jet is signed by the team. A must-have for the ultimate Kings fan: $5,000,000.

Heck, for $5,000,000 a baseball franchise could almost buy the services of a starting pitcher for one season.

I'm saving the catalog just in case any of you win the Florida lottery and would like to order some of this stuff.

But I have one question: What do you do with it after you buy it?

PART THREE

THE GOOD OLD DAYS
KEEP GETTING BETTER

I think it's true that "the older a man gets, the faster he could run as a boy."

Ahhhhhhh! The good old days. When were they? The 1790s? The 1820s? The 1940s? I don't know. I do know that the more I hear about them, the better they become.

I have some great memories of the so-called good old days. I also have some that are not so great—like outdoor toilets on a cold and rainy winter night or early morning; cold as ice linoleum floors; chopping fireplace wood; working in a grocery store all day Saturday for two dollars; growing up as an only child; the jungles of the South Pacific; malaria; being jilted by a girlfriend and being beaten to a pulp by her new boyfriend; divorce; an empty wallet; an old used car but no money for gas; and being in New York City alone, broke, and hungry. If those were the good old days, you can have them.

In this section I have tried to shed some light on where we were and how far we've come. Like with memories of cars in the forties and fifties, and trying to buy one; the evolution of the telephone; things saved over the years; and how many things have changed in the past thirty years.

I try not to live in the past, but I sure as heck don't mind glancing backward now and then. I heard an old man explain once why as a boy he always rode sitting backward on the wagon when his daddy took the family to town on Saturday for the weekly shopping: "I really never cared where I was going. I just wanted to see where I'd been."

I have great memories. I have no intention of ever trying to blot them out. After all, aren't memories what dreams are made of?

OLD ADDICTIONS ARE HARD TO KICK

A man does not easily admit that he's behaved foolishly. In most cases he will deny it, even to himself, until the realization comes and he seeks professional help or self-induced rehabilitation.

I have been an addict. Pure and simple. There are no other words to describe it. As a matter of fact, I have suffered through several bouts of addiction. I think I'm clean now. I hope so.

• Back in my younger days as a grammar school student, I became addicted to Hershey's Kisses, also known as Silver Bells. Most days I arrived at school with a pocketful of the little candy morsels shaped like a bell, wrapped in tin foil, with a white and blue paper Hershey's flag sticking out of the top.

I bought Hershey's kisses during the thirties and early forties for a now unbelievable price: five for a penny or twenty-five for a nickel. I even kept buying them after becoming a grown man and absorbed a rate increase. They were standard fare in my house, kept in a candy jar on the coffee table.

I took the cure recently when I reached for a handful in a convenience store before reading the price: five cents each or five for a quarter!

• I was also addicted to Mr. Goodbars for years. I still love and eat them, but in moderation.

For years I bought Mr. Goodbars by the box (twenty-four) and kept a box on my car seat and another under my bed. I would easily go through ten Mr. Goodbars a day. I wasn't "Looking for Mr. Goodbar"; I found him and stayed with him for a long, long time.

• I was also a TV addict in the fifties and sixties, hooked on programs like "The Ed Sullivan Show," "The Honeymooners," "Twilight Zone," "Sergeant Bilko," "All in the Family," "The Andy Griffith Show," "The Dick

Van Dyke Show," and "The Tonight Show."

I started with Steve Allen on "The Tonight Show" and he and his regulars were welcome guests in my living room. Let's see, there were Don Knotts, Tom Poston, Gordon Hathaway, Andy Williams, Steve Lawrence, Eydie Gorme, and others.

I stayed with the show through the Jack Paar era and still can't imagine Paar being kicked off the air by NBC censors for making reference to a "water closet" (English bathroom) on the air when I look at all the trash and scum that clutters the tube today. (Remember all the fuss over whether or not to allow Elvis to appear on "The Ed Sullivan Show" because of his pelvic gyrations? He appeared, and the viewers fell in love with him. Elvis's moves were mild compared to what you can see today on "Soul Train.")

My longest addiction, but easiest to break, was "The Tonight Show" starring Johnny Carson. Carson tucked me in bed every night for thirty years until I kicked "The Tonight Show" in 1992. That's when Leno crashed the gate of "The Tonight Show" studio in Burbank, California, after Johnny Carson hung it up.

One night of Leno cured me and I haven't watched the show since. I switched totally to CNN.

● Two other things to which I was totally addicted were hard to overcome: college football on Saturday afternoon and professional football on Sunday afternoon. I grew up with both. I ran with them, tackled with them, passed with them, punted with them, received with them, kicked extra points and field goals with them, and won and lost with them. But no more.

I have now kicked the habit. I'm no longer an addict to the football fever. My pigskin fever is now back to normal. It wasn't easy, but I kicked the habit during the "1992 Football Follies," formerly known as "The 1992 Football Season."

THE PHONE HAS COME A LONG WAY, OR HAS IT?

Have you ever considered the evolution of the telephone? I've been doing that for several years and find it to be quite interesting.

I started out with a crank phone. Just turn the crank, like trying to crank a Model T Ford, and tell the operator the desired number. The telephone at my house, in Lumpkin, Georgia, was one that had the receiver detached from the part you talked into. It took two hands to operate it.

Next came the streamlined (in the early forties) phone with the receiver and the thing you talked into attached to the same gadget. You still gave the operator the desired number. We were also on a party line (two longs and a short). The party line was my prime source of recreation and information as a teenager.

The dial phone followed. I thought that was the most streamlined thing I ever saw. Just dial the number and sooner or later your party answered.

Direct dialing almost blew my mind. I still don't know how it works.

Many more innovations followed.

Now, as to telephone numbers, we have come full circle. You've seen 'em, the 1-800-WORD numbers. Like WSB radio features 1-800-WSB-TALK instead of 1-800-972-8255 if you want to call the "Ludlow Porch Show." The American Beef Council touts 1-800-EAT-BEEF. The National Drug Hotline answers to 1-800-NO-DRUGS. Call 1-800-AIM-FIRE and get the National Rifle Association; 1-800-RIGHT-ON and listen to a rock band; or 1-800-I'M-BROKE could get you a savings and loan. The secret to all these is seven letters following the 800 that replace the numbers.

Some of the kinky 800 numbers are misleading, however. I found this out on a recent Tuesday night when I turned on my television set anticipating a baseball game between the Atlanta Braves and the Cincinnati Reds. This is what came on the screen: 1-800-FLOWERS. I was amazed. Had Gennifer gotten her own 800 number and turned pro? I had to give it a try, at no charge, of course.

I dialed the 800 number and waited. Shortly, a soft, sweet voice answered, "Flowers, may I help you?"

"Yeah, is this Gennifer?" I asked.

"No, this is Marlene."

"Can I speak to Gennifer?"

"I'm sorry, but there is no Gennifer here, sir."

"Is this 1-800-FLOWERS?"

"That's right," Marlene said.

"Do you make house calls?"

"Oh, yes! Anywhere in the United States and most foreign countries," Marlene cooed.

"Well, send Gennifer to my house in Dublin, Georgia, 119 North Elm Street."

"There must be some mistake," Marlene said.

"Well, is this Gennifer Flowers' house?"

"Oh, no, sir. This is the Clinton Flower Shop in Clinton, Arkansas, a member of FTD Florists."

Drat it! Just my luck, I thought. But I really shouldn't have been surprised because back when Elizabeth Taylor was in her prime, before she got old and fat, I picked up the telephone and called "Butterfield 8" in great anticipation. Richard Burton answered.

A telephone repairman, who had just installed some new equipment in the Pentagon, got lost when trying to leave the building. Finally, thoroughly confused, he ducked into an office and yelled to the girl seated at the switchboard:

"How the heck do I get outside?"

"Simple. Just dial 9," snapped the girl busily.

Food for Thought: If Alexander Graham Bell had had a teenage daughter he never would have had a chance to test the telephone.

REMEMBER WHAT IT WAS LIKE WHEN?

L ike many of you, I watched the political shenanigans that went on for months in 1992, and I'm sorta glad it's over up there. Now the country can go back into hibernation for another four years.

The more I listened to all the rhetoric and America-bashing, the more I wondered what ever happened to the real America. Today, it just ain't the same. Do you remember what it was like . . .

- When riots were unthinkable?
- When ghettos were neighborhoods?
- When the American flag was a sacred symbol?
- When you weren't afraid to walk the streets alone at night?
- When all schools had chapel programs every morning?
- When a boy was a boy, and dressed like one?
- When a girl was a girl, and dressed like one?
- (When you could actually tell the difference?)
- When blue jeans were work pants?
- When the poor were too proud to accept charity?
- When songs had a tune and the words made sense?
- When it never crossed your mind that America could lose?
- When people expected less and valued what they had more?
- When couples married for keeps and held on to each other "until death do us part"?
- When divorce was considered a community disaster?
- When the ACLU was unheard of?
- When the Bible was read in the classroom?
- When you could attend a movie with your mother and have no fear that either of you would be embarrassed or insulted?
- When families were honored to have the preacher

and his family for Sunday dinner?

- When manual labor was honorable and dirty hands were acceptable?
- When people knew all of their obligations as well as their rights?
- When sick people took drugs to restore their health as opposed to today when healthy people take drugs to destroy it?
- When the only babysitter a child ever knew was Mama?
- When everybody ran outside to look when an airplane went over?
- When families came to town on Saturday, visited all day, and stores stayed open until midnight?
- When Daddy really did wear the pants in the family?
- When doors were left unlocked and you had no fear of intruders?
- When *socialism* was a dirty word?
- When *gay* meant carefree and happy?

- When convicted criminals actually went to prison?
- When clerks and repairmen tried hard to please you?
- When everybody didn't feel entitled to a college education?
- When things weren't perfect, but then you never expected them to be?
- When policemen were respected?
- When the law meant justice?
- When teachers taught and students listened and got their backsides tanned for misbehavior with no fear by the teacher of being hauled into court?
- When the best trip was going to see Grandma and Grandpa?

I remember it, all of it. To me it was great America. But where did it go? I think we desperately need to find it, and soon.

HOW CARS WERE SOLD
IN THE GOOD OLD DAYS

One topic that's at the top of the news these days is the economy. Most agree that it is in shambles and getting worse. Millions are out of work and the employment offices are overflowing.

Along with the economy, and tied closely to it, is the automobile industry and lagging sales. President Bush even went to Japan, along with the heads of General Motors, Ford, and Chrysler, to try to sell a few thousand.

Will the Japanese import American cars? Only if the Japanese will buy them, and they've shown little interest.

On the other hand, American buyers have taken to Japanese cars like a duck to water. As a result the American automobile dealers are now offering more incentives and rebates to potential car buyers than a presidential candidate, Democrat or Republican. But it wasn't always that way, and that's what I want to talk about.

Let's go back to 1946 and 1947. That was just after World War II and new cars were all but impossible to buy. Every dealer had a list as long as a railroad track, and a customer almost had to beg to buy a car. Some of you will have no idea what I'm talking about, but some of you are as old as I am and will.

Here's the way car buying worked just after the war.

I was very fortunate. I arrived back home from the Philippine Islands in November 1946, at the ripe old age of nineteen and was able to purchase my first car, a 1947 Chevrolet Fleetline, in January 1947.

The Chevrolet dealer in Metter, George Franklin, promised me that I would get a car shortly after I returned home from the war. He was true to his word. And not only that, he sold it to me at list price: $1,334.50. Buying a new car at list price was highly unusual.

I picked up my new car shortly before noon, drove to my father's house, and parked it in the front yard. My first car! I just sat on the porch and admired it. Guess what? While I was sitting there, another dealer drove up, walked up on the porch, and offered me $2,400 for the car. No sale. I wouldn't have sold it for any amount of money. And I will always be indebted to George Franklin.

Several months later my father was notified by another dealer in another town that his car had arrived and he could pick it up the next morning—at 3:00 A.M.! It worked this way:

The dealer had received three cars. He had them hidden in the woods some twelve miles from town. He told my father to meet him at an all-night service station at 2:30 A.M., and he would show us the way.

We did as instructed and followed the dealer into deep woods where three Chevrolets were covered with brush. The transaction was made on the hood of the dealer's pickup. My father drove his new car back to Metter after promising the dealer that he wouldn't tell anyone where he got the car.

That's the way it was back then. No incentives, no rebates, and no Japanese cars. And I believe more cars were sold from the woods than from the showrooms.

FOR THOSE BORN BEFORE 1945

If you were born before 1945, chances are you can relate to this chapter. I was and I can.

For All Those Born before 1945

We are survivors! Consider the changes we have witnessed:

- We were born before television, before penicillin, before polio shots, frozen foods, Xerox, contact lenses, 7-11 stores and "the pill."
- We were born before pantyhose, automatic dishwashers, clothes dryers, electric blankets, air conditioning, drip-dry clothing, and before man walked on the moon.
- We got married first and lived together afterward.
- Closets were for clothes, not "coming out of." Bunnies were small rabbits, and rabbits were not Volkswagens.
- Designer jeans were scheming girls named Jean or Jeannie, and having a "meaningful relationship" meant getting along well with our cousins on both sides of the family.
- Fast food was what you ate during Lent, and outer space was the back of the local theater.
- We were before househusbands, gay rights, computer dating, dual careers, and palimony suits.
- We were before day care centers, group therapy, and nursing homes.
- We never heard of FM radio, tape decks, electric typewriters, artificial hearts and by-passes, word processors, yogurt, guys wearing earrings, and cholesterol.
- Time-sharing meant togetherness and visiting neighbors, not condominiums.
- We were before computers, and "chip" meant a piece of wood. Software meant clean diapers.
- "Made in Japan" meant a piece of junk, and the term "making out" referred to how we did on an exam.

• Pizzas, McDonald's, and instant coffee were unheard of.

• "Rock" was something you threw in the creek, and "cool" was a glass of ice water on a hot day in July or August.

• There were five-and-ten-cent stores where you actually bought things for five and ten cents. For a nickel you could buy a Coke, make a telephone call, or get enough stamps to mail a letter and two postcards.

• You could buy a new Ford or Chevrolet for $600, but who could afford one? A pity, too, what with gasoline only eleven cents a gallon.

• Cigarette smoking was fashionable, grass was mowed, Coke was a soft drink, and pot was something you cooked in or it sat under the edge of the bed.

• Rock music was Grandma's lullaby, and aids were helpers in the principal's office.

• We were before sex change; we made do with what we had. And we were the last generation so dumb as to think you needed a husband to have a baby.

But somehow . . . we survived.

—Author Unknown

Here are a few more that come to mind:

• Doctors made house calls and were darn glad to get the business.

• Males didn't have their hair styled in a salon; they had it cut in a barbershop.

• Preachers visited the sick, and no appointment was necessary to see one in his office.

• A "high five" was a covey of quail flying overhead, and businessmen sealed a deal with a handshake, not a "high five." Somehow, I just can't see a "high five" as binding.

• Men wore pants and women wore dresses.

• People went to Sunday night church and Wednesday night prayer meeting.

A BACKWARD GLANCE, FIFTY YEARS AGO

With the passing of 1992, the comparison to previous years is inevitable. I made the comparison Saturday, January 2, as I browsed in my recliner. It doesn't take long for fifty years to pass when you do it in the comfort of a recliner in front of a fireplace. Actually, I dozed off somewhere between 1957 and 1963.

I compared 1992 to the highs and lows of forty or fifty years ago, like 1942–50. Here they are:

1942

- Fell in love with Margaret Purvis. I was fifteen; she was thirty-three. She was my social studies teacher. I'm pretty sure Margaret never knew I existed outside her roll book. At the end of the school year in June, she married the basketball coach. I've never completely gotten over that. Broken hearts don't mend easily.
- Went to Atlanta for the first time. Slept in a hotel room for the first time at the Henry Grady—$3.00.

I was absolutely amazed at room service. Me and the king of England, Clark Gable, or Spencer Tracy.

1943

- Graduated from high school and went on the senior trip to New Orleans and Washington, two worlds I didn't know existed.
- Saw a stripper, Lily Christine, "the Cat Girl," in New Orleans. I was scared to death for fear that Margaret Purvis would find out about it. I think I fell in love with Lily, too.
- Entered junior college.

1944

- Graduated from junior college.
- Went in the U.S. Army at the invitation of President Roosevelt.

1945

- Vacationed for eighteen months in the Philippine Islands. All expenses paid by my rich uncle—Sam.
- Saw my first and only

cockfight. It was sickening.

• Spent the loneliest
Christmas ever in the 4th
General Hospital in Manila.
Malaria. I was too dumb to
sleep under a mosquito net
on the island of Leyte.

1946

• Stood with thousands on
July 4th, in Manila, and
heard General Douglas Mac-
Arthur deliver the speech
granting the Philippine Islands their independence.

• Returned to the U.S.A in
October aboard the USS *West
Point*. Got seasick. Wanted to
die. Afraid I wouldn't.

• Discharged at Fort Sam
Houston, Texas, the morning
of November 3. General
Jonathan Wainwright did the
honors.

• Spent the only night of
my life in jail in San An-
tonio, Texas, the night of
November 3. Details aren't
important, but I can tell you
that while oil and water
won't mix, neither will
Southern Comfort, Coke, and
a nineteen-year-old imbibing
virgin trying hard to prove
his manhood. I learned a
great lesson, for which I am
thankful to this day. No more
liquor. I've never revealed
this before.

1947

• Bought my first auto-
mobile, a 1947 Chevrolet
Fleetline, Sierra Suntan and
San Pedro Ivory. It was the
most beautiful car I'd ever
seen. I almost washed and
polished the paint off it the
first week I had it. The price,
incidentally, was $1,334.50. I
still have the bill of sale.

1948

• Entered Georgia Teachers
College in January.

• Played baseball and basketball, and a little poker.

1949

• Graduated from Georgia
Teachers College in June.

• Signed my first profes-
sional baseball contract and
reported to the Dublin Green
Sox. Figured I'd be with the
Yankees or Red Sox in a
couple of weeks. Need I elab-
orate? I had fun in the minor
leagues for six years.

• Reported for my first
teaching and coaching job at
Georgia Military College in
September.

• Hmmm. Let's see. I did
something else in 1949. Oh,
yeah. I got married.

Not much has happened
since 1949.

THINGS SAVED OVER THE YEARS

As a saver, jotter-downer, and passage-marker I save copies of foolishness, jot down things for future reference, and underline sentences.

Some people would never write in a book. I write all over the pages, and dog-ear them, but only my own. Here are a few of the things saved, jotted down, underlined, or dog eared:

Cow for sale: The farmer had been ripped off by a car dealer. When the dealer approached him about buying a cow, he priced it to him like this:

- Basic cow—$200.
- Two-tone—$45.
- Extra stomach—$75.
- Storage compartment—$60.
- Dispensing devices—Four spigots at $10 each equals $40.
- Genuine cowhide upholstery—$125.
- Dual horns—$75.
- Fly swatter—$35.
Total price—$695.

A few hits and misses from the baseball world:
- "All right, everybody, line up in alphabetical order according to your height" (Casey Stengel, instructing his players during spring training).
- "Ninety percent of this game is half mental" (Jim Wohlford, former major-league outfielder during postgame interview).
- "America is the greatest country in the United States" (St. Louis Cardinals sportscaster Mike Shannon before a July 4th double-header).
- "We have to avoid swinging and missing" (Joe Torre, during a clubhouse meeting while manager of the St. Louis Cardinals).

Here's a letter from a corporate executive in Macon after requesting and receiving several copies of my book:

Dear Bo,
  Thanks for sending the books. They have helped me and my family understand life in the South a lot better.
  I never thought of myself as a Yankee until I moved to Georgia. That's because the term *Yankee* is relative; and even though I'm from Boston, I don't qualify.
  Here's my mother's definition of a Yankee that explains why I'm *not* a Yankee:
  To a foreigner a Yankee is an American.
  To an American a Yankee is a Northerner.
  To a Northerner a Yankee is a New Englander.
  To a New Englander a Yankee is a Vermonter.
  To a Vermonter a Yankee is someone who . . .
  Eats apple pie for breakfast!
                                    Best wishes,
                                    Stephen L. White, Ph.D.

After Earth Day each year, I'm always amazed the earth has survived. And lest you think land erosion is a recent concern, take a look at this item that appeared in the Danbury (Connecticut) *News-Times* forty years ago.

The editor printed a picture of a deserted and rundown farmhouse in a desolate, sandswept field, then offered a prize for the best one hundred-word essay on the disastrous effects of land erosion.

A bright Indian lad from Oklahoma bagged the trophy with this graphic description:

"Picture show white man crazy. Cut down trees. Make too big tepee. Plow hill. Water wash. Wind blow soil. Grass gone. Door gone. Squaw gone. Whole place gone to hell. No pig. No corn. No pony.

"Indian no plow land. Keep grass. Buffalo eat grass. Indian eat buffalo. Hide make plenty big tepee. Make moccasins. All time Indian eat. No work. No hitchhike. No ask relief. No build dam. White man heap crazy."

THINGS SURE HAVE CHANGED IN THIRTY YEARS

A lthough I don't watch a lot of television, in the last year I have watched more than I've watched in the past thirty years. Conclusion: I haven't missed much.

CNN must have thousands of analysts and experts in cages and can summon one to analyze or comment on any given subject. And how many female talk show hosts are there? Hundreds, no doubt. Apparently their objective is to see just how much thigh they can expose without getting arrested.

There's a cable channel called C-Span. It is apparently on the tube to give politicians free television time. I watched it very little, but when I did I heard the darndest exhibition of double-talk ever. To paraphrase Winston Chuchill, never have so many said so much to say so little.

I watched a lot of news on CNN. CNN has all but taken over the news business, leaving Dan Rather, Peter Jennings, and the rest of the network anchors in the dust.

For most of December 1992 the news was mostly about Russia and the fall of Mikhail Gorbachev, along with the pitiful and hopeless expressions on the faces of the Russian people. Also the bare shelves in Russian grocery stores and the long lines waiting to get inside to maybe buy a loaf of bread or a piece of meat. I visited a Dublin supermarket last week; and as I strolled the aisles, saw shopping carts piled high, and checked the prices of the goods on the shelves, I thought about the price of groceries thirty years ago. I drove to the *Courier Herald* and spent about an hour in the morgue checking prices in January 1962. While they seem unbelievable today, some of you will no doubt remember them.

- Cokes. Regular Size. Six-bottle Carton. 15 cents.

- Large Eggs. 47 cents dozen.

- Sunset Gold Bread. Loaf 10 cents.
- Ground Beef. Three pounds 99 cents.
- Green Beans. 10 cents a can.
- Campbells Tomato Soup. 10 cents a can.
- Catsup. 14 Oz. bottle. 15 cents.
- Apple Juice. Quart 25 cents.
- Bananas. 10 cents a pound.
- Mayonnaise. Quart 39 cents.
- Maxwell House Coffee. Pound 49 cents.
- Grapefruit. 8 pounds 49 cents.
- Flour. 25-pound bag $1.89.
- Milk. 8 tall cans $1.00.
- Chicken Pot Pies. 4 for 69 cents.
- Evaporated milk. Tall can 9 cents.
- Sliced bacon. 39 cents pound.
- White Meat Tuna. 33 cents a can.
- Scott Tissue. 9 cents a roll.
- Pork Chops. 3 pounds for $1.00.
- Jello. 7 cents a package.
- Apples. 5-pound bag 39 cents.
- Apple Sauce. 17 cents a can.
- Kleenex. 9 cents a box.
- Slab Bacon. 39 cents a pound.
- 100 St. Joseph Aspirin. 59 cents.
- Fab. Large box 29 cents.
- Lux or Palmolive Soap. 2 bars for 21 cents.
- Peanut Butter. 2-pound jar 29 cents.
- Pork and Beans. 10 oz. can 5 cents.
- T-Bone or Sirloin Steak. 69 cents a pound.
- Delmonte Peaches. 19 cents a can.
- Oranges. 23 cents a dozen.
- Fryers. 29 cents a pound.
- Dixie Crystal Sugar. 5 pounds 35 cents.
- Raisin Bread. 2 one-pound loaves 39 cents.
- Mullet fish. 10 cents a pound.
- Jim Dandy Grits. One-pound package 8 cents.
- Jergens Lotion. Large bottle 59 cents.
- Ice Cream. ½ gallon 49 cents.

There were three other items, not in the grocery line, that caught my eye.

- Sweat Shirts. 69 cents.
- Electric Blankets. $10.84.
- Handkerchiefs. 10 for 88 cents.

PART FOUR

IF WOMEN ARE THE OPPOSITE SEX, WHAT ARE MEN?

One of the very few original things I've ever said is, "I don't really have much time for women; but I have all the time in the world for ladies." And there *is* a difference.

The ages of my female friends range from three to ninety-two. I cherish every one of them.

The Persian poet Armand Saadi wrote in one of his sixteenth-century epistles what in my opinion is a classic line regarding the female of the species: "A handsome woman is a jewel; a good woman is a treasure."

How right Saadi was!

A woman can make a man completely happy on the one hand or completely miserable on the other. They are to be loved and tolerated, pampered and protected, held and shielded. And they should come one to a customer. You know, " . . . only unto her as long as ye both shall live." Corny? I hope not.

Women can and will blow your mind with their logic. Forget the details. The end result is what women look for.

If I have a favorite subject about which I write, it is women. They are unpredictable, but fun. It has been said that the only way to fight a woman is with your hat. Grab it and run!

I can stand my ground with any woman alive until she starts crying. That gets to me.

Here in this section I have included some great experiences with the opposite sex (in this case, women). I dearly love to watch them to see what unpredictable thing they will do next. In any confrontation with a woman, I invariably lose. But the confrontation is so much fun.

I can't possibly imagine a world without women. I love women. My dear mother was one, a great one. I owe her a deep debt of gratitude because where would I be without her? She brought me here, and I try every day to remember to try hard not to disappoint her. I'm not the judge as to the degree of my success.

Legend has it that a newspaper reporter who was interviewing Sir Winston Churchill asked, "What do you say, sir, to the prediction that in the year 2000 women will be ruling the world?"

Churchill smiled his characteristic smile and replied, "They still will, eh?"

THE MARRIAGE BOMB EXPLODES

I hadn't heard a bomb explode in forty-five years until a recent morning when one went off in the newsroom at the *Courier Herald*.

The explosion came at precisely 9:28 A.M., according to the wall clock. I dropped my cup of coffee and rammed my nose in a raspberry Danish clear up to my eyebrows. That's how scary it was.

I had made my usual morning stop in the newsroom and overheard but a portion of the conversation already in progress when I arrived. The subject was marriage.

Somebody had married recently, and the reporters were discussing it. Then, the bomb exploded when I heard somebody say, "and I think Bo Whaley ought to get married, too!"

I said nothing in rebuttal but picked up my cup, wiped my nose, and walked to the coffee room to consider what I had heard. Me? Married? No way, I thought. That's as remote as Ted Kennedy becoming a driving instructor. I'm as single-spaced as a typewriter. But I did give the matter of marriage serious thought.

I concluded that marriage possibly had some merit. Like togetherness, a traveling companion on long trips, home cooking, clean sheets, no need for a telephone answering machine, buttered toast for breakfast, and all that jazz. Why not?

I reached for a sheet of paper and drafted a classified ad: "Wanted: Female for better or worse. Must be tolerant. Prefer sensual millionaire who owns liquor store."

Finished, I walked over to advertising intent on placing the ad. I never made it to the classified desk. A burst of red stopped me cold as I walked through the doorway.

There she sat, talking on the telephone between bites of a hamburger and sips of Coke, a pretty redhead.

I ripped the ad to shreds, walked to her desk, and waited for her to finish talking, eating, and drinking. Then I made my pitch in my usual suave and debonair manner.

"Uh . . . I was wonderin' if you might be free at three o'clock Friday afternoon," I said.

"Friday? At three?" she said. "Why?"

"Oh, I jus' thought if you weren't tied up maybe you'd like to get married," I said.

"Married? To whom?"

"Me."

(Dead silence.)

"Hmmmmmmm . . . Friday at three," she repeated. "I doubt it. You see, Bo, Friday afternoons are pretty busy for me. I have to pull all my tear sheets and go to my grocery store accounts. I don't think I can make it. Also, I'd have to go shopping for a dress. I don't see how I could work it all in. Ask me another time, okay?"

"Okay, another time," I said and, like the rich young ruler, turned away sorrowfully.

I asked her again on Wednesday, Friday, and Monday. On each occasion I was still playing second fiddle to tear sheets and grocery stores.

I don't give up easily.

A couple of random quotes on marriage:

• "Me and my wife go fifty-fifty on everything: I tell her what to do and she tells me where to go."

• Woman to the clerk at a fur shop: "Will a small deposit hold it until I catch my husband doing something unforgivable?"

• Wife to husband: "You certainly made a fool of yourself at the party last night. I only hope no one realized you were sober."

• "Do you and your wife ever have a difference of opinion?" a friend asked.

"Darn right. But I don't tell her about it."

• "If it weren't for marriage, people could go through life thinking they had no faults at all."

• "Home is where the husband runs the show, but the wife writes the script."

• "The perfect marriage would be between a blind wife and a deaf husband."

MOTHER SPILLS THE BEANS ON DAUGHTER AFTER THIRTY YEARS

Mothers are loyal. You can take that to the bank. Mothers can keep a secret, especially one entrusted to her by her daughter.

The confidential relationship that exists between mother and daughter far outweighs the confidentiality of the time-honored and respected lawyer/client, patient/doctor, psychiatrist/patient, priest/parishioner relationship.

A daughter will share secrets with her mother that she wouldn't dare tell her priest. And in most cases, *most* cases, her secret is as safe as if she'd revealed it to the Price Waterhouse accounting firm that keeps the identity of Miss America under lock and key in a sealed envelope every September.

But there are exceptions:

On Christmas Eve, shortly before noon I stopped by the office of a good friend, Leo, to deliver a small Christmas remembrance as I do every Christmas. He's that good a friend, as is his pretty wife, Myra.

"Thank you," Leo said. "By the way, what are you doing for lunch?"

"No plans," I said.

"Good. How about joining Myra and me? Her mother is visiting with us this Christmas, and I'm meeting them here at the office in a few minutes. We're going to the country club for lunch and would love to have you join us," he said.

"Great," I replied. "I'd love to see Miss Ophelia. She's a lovely lady. I have a couple of errands to run, so why don't I take care of those on the way and meet you at the club in about twenty minutes?"

"That'll be fine," Leo agreed. "We'll see you there."

While it wasn't in the script, I might mention here that I

glanced at my fuel gauge after leaving Leo's office. It was on the big "E." "No problem," I said to myself. "There's *always* a couple of gallons left. The automobile manufacturers see to that." Wrong! The automobile manufacturers don't always see to that. My car died from malnutrition two miles from the country club. I arrived forty-five minutes late and joined Leo, Myra, and Miss Ophelia who were well into their desserts and second cups of coffee. Leo was into his third Kool. I offered my apologies, took a seat in the lone remaining chair at the table, and scanned the menu. I ordered chicken fingers. Did you know that chickens have fingers? Toes, yes. But fingers? I didn't question it.

The four of us then engaged in the normal small talk that accompanies lunch with good friends, and somehow the conversation drifted to my eating habits. Leo is very much aware that I'm a picky eater, as is he, and pointed out to Miss Ophelia that there are certain things of which I absolutely refuse to partake, like liver.

"No, ma'am," I said to Miss Ophelia. "I don't eat liver, or nothin' else that bloats, secretes, quivers, shivers, has whiskers, crawls, lives in a hole in the ground, climbs trees, or looks back at me while stretched out on a platter. Liver! I've left more liver untouched on my plate as a dinner guest than Morrison's Cafeteria ever cooked."

"I'm with you, Bo. Ugh! I can't stand the thought of eating liver," Myra said, thereby verifying that she is equally as intelligent as she is pretty. "But Leo loves it! Liver and onions is his favorite dish."

I wonder how Leo, the liver lover, ever made it through law school because liver ain't exactly no brain food.

The mere mention of liver prompted Miss Ophelia to relate the following. In doing so she completely blew Myra out of the water by revealing a secret that Myra had shared with her thirty years previously. While Miss Ophelia is ninety years young, she's as lively and frisky as a young doe and, much to Myra's disdain, has a steel-trap mind and a computer-type memory.

Here's the story as she told it while Myra squirmed in obvious discomfort and Leo lit up another Kool. He listened intently with more than a passing interest—as did I.

Myra's Thirty-Year Secret Revealed

Back in the early sixties, Leo and Myra lived in the Buckhead section of Atlanta. He was a student at Georgia State University. She was a young housewife.

Leo repeatedly pleaded with his young bride to cook liver and onions for him on weekends. She repeatedly balked at the idea but had a brainstorm one day and offered to make a deal with Leo, who steadfastly refused to attend church on Sunday mornings—preferring the Sunday newspaper, coffee, and a few Kools, feeling that Sunday mornings were a time for browsing and end of the week relaxation.

Leo, by the way, was and is somewhat bullheaded: a trademark of the legal society. Myra, while not bullheaded, was and is shrewd and cunning. Most schoolteachers have to be.

"I'll tell you what I'll do, Leo," the conniving Myra said. "If you'll go to church, I'll serve liver and onions every Sunday for lunch." (Please note the key word here: *serve*.)

"All right, it's a deal," Leo agreed.

At this point, Myra interrupted Miss Ophelia. "Mother! You aren't going to—?"

Hah! Miss Ophelia was on a roll. No stopping her.

What Leo failed to realize was that near their apartment, within walking distance, was a very nice cafeteria, one that served liver and onions every Sunday! And no sooner would he leave the apartment on Sunday morning than Myra would hot-foot it to the cafeteria and buy—what else?—liver and onions for Leo's lunch.

"Myra did this for four years, and Leo never suspected a thing," Miss Ophelia said. "Liver and onions every Sunday."

Again, Myra interrupted. "Mother! How could you do such a thing? After thirty years you have violated a coveted confidence between us!"

Undaunted, Miss Ophelia nibbled on her dessert and said, "Well, my goodness, Myra! I thought that surely you would have told Leo about your scheme by now. And if you haven't, I think he deserves to know. So there!"

Leo said nothing. He just fingered his Kool and tried in vain to maintain his cool. Finally, "You mean you didn't cook that liver and onions?"

Myra, on the verge of tears, responded with, "No! I didn't! But you had your liver and onions every Sunday, and at least I got you to go to church! So there!"

Now it was my turn to interrupt and violate the age-old, cardinal rule of never intervening in a family dispute.

"Myra, I know Leo pretty darn well, and I'll just guarantee you that while you were at the cafeteria buying that liver and onions, he wasn't singing hymns and reading Responsive Readings in church," I allowed.

"Oh? Where was he then if he wasn't in church?" she asked.

"In that little coffee shop that was about three blocks from your apartment, in the opposite direction from the cafeteria— reading the Sunday paper, drinking coffee, and smoking a few Kools!"

Myra flashed a killing look at Leo, and squealed, "Is that true?"

Drawing on his legal expertise, Leo drew on his Kool and replied, "I'm seeking, as it is my legal right to do, protection under the Fifth Amendment."

Then, a sense of alarming realization hit Myra like a bolt of lightning. "You aren't going to write about this, are you?" she asked in an almost pleading voice.

"No sooner than I can get to my typewriter," I assured her.

"Oh, my goodness!" she exclaimed. "You wouldn't identify us by name, would you?"

"Never," I promised.

"And not with any identifying phrases or descriptions?" asked Leo.

"I'm seeking, as it is my legal right to do, protection under the Fifth Amendment," I said.

I may well have lost two good friends by writing this, but it is proof that a dedicated writer knows no bounds when it comes to gathering material. We just ain't got no scruples.

HOUSEWIFE TAKES FULL ADVANTAGE OF OPPORTUNITY

When an opportunity presents itself, seize upon it, I always say. And there is a pretty housewife in Dublin who subscribes to the same theory. Here's the story related to me by her husband. Knowing him, it may or may not be true; but for now I'll accept it as fact and check it out with his wife later.

I was socializing with a group of friends when one, the husband who told me this story, received this message from his wife: "Come home immediately." He did what any husband in his right mind would have done; he went home immediately.

After about an hour had passed, those of us still socializing became increasingly concerned and called his home to determine if everything was all right. We were pleased to hear that there was no big problem, just a small grease fire in the kitchen that had caused minor damage.

A few days later I was in conversation with the husband and again asked if everything was all right at home. He assured me that it was, that the insurance adjuster had been there and done his thing, and plans to repair the damage were under way. But he told me something else, and therein lies the story.

"The insurance adjuster hadn't been gone two minutes when Charlotte (not her real name) began making plans," Eugene (not his real name) said.

"What do you mean?" I asked.

"Well, first she said she wanted to replace the burned kitchen counter with a beige one," Eugene said. "I agreed that the counter needed to be replaced and that beige was fine with me."

"Then she said she wanted to replace the cabinets with ones to match the beige counter. I voiced no objection, picked up the newspaper, and began reading," Eugene said. "But Charlotte kept walking around looking in the kitchen and breakfast room areas. Finally, she said that she thought the rug in the breakfast room should be replaced and asked if I preferred a round or rectangular one. I expressed no preference, figuring that I could walk on and spill food on either."

According to Eugene, Charlotte wasn't finished. Sensing her opportunity, she moved over near the sofa and two chairs in the den.

"She mused over the sofa and chairs briefly before concluding that they should be replaced, with something to match the rug, counter top, and cabinets. While she was moving farther and farther away from the kitchen," Eugene said, "I was standing at the back door getting ready to go to town when I heard her say, 'You know something, Eugene, I never have particularly liked the color of the curtains in this room. I think I'll . . .' and I left."

On his way to his car, Eugene spotted a small weathered spot on the back of the house, up near the eaves, about the size of a medium pizza. He wouldn't dare mention it to Charlotte. Why?

"Because I'm pretty sure the adjuster's recommendation as to compensation won't be sufficient to have the house painted," Eugene said. "In fact, I'm not too sure about the sofa, chairs, and the curtains."

Hang in there, Eugene, and keep your fingers crossed that the television or microwave doesn't start acting up. And the central air conditioning unit? Don't even think about that.

It's amazing what a small grease fire can do. It could cause an entire house to be refurnished, remodeled, and painted, including the mailbox out front.

DUMB BLONDE JOKE FAD HAS FIZZLED OUT

Whatever happened to all the dumb blonde jokes? They roared in like a lion and then tiptoed out like a lamb a few months later.

I never particularly liked the blonde jokes myself, for several reasons:

- My favorite girl in the world is a blonde. She lives in Macon. I call her Lisa, and she calls me Daddy. And she ain't dumb.
- Another blonde I know lives in Augusta with her lucky husband, David, and their two children. She's beautiful. I've been in love with her for more than ten years, since she was in high school. I call her Susan, and she calls me Bo.
- I've never understood what the color of a female's hair has to do with the degree of her intelligence underneath it.

But I have to stop and realize that Madonna is a blonde. So is Zsa Zsa, if further evidence is needed.

I have a good friend in Dublin, a blonde, who despises blonde jokes. Her son loves 'em. She gave me a list some of the more popular ones he gave her. Maybe you've heard 'em. Maybe you ain't. If you're a blonde and have heard 'em, maybe you've forgotten 'em. Here are a few.

- What do you call a refrigerator full of blondes?
  Frosted Flakes.
- What do you call a blonde with half a brain?
  Gifted.
- How do you confuse a blonde?
  Hand her a bag of M&Ms and tell her to put them in alphabetical order.
- How do you know that a blonde has been working at your computer?
  When there's White-Out all over the screen.
- What do blondes and beer bottles have in common?
  Both are empty from the neck up.

• What do you do when a blonde throws a hand grenade at you?

Pull the pin and throw it back.

• What's the advantage of being married to a blonde?

You can park in a handicapped zone.

• How do you make a blonde laugh on Monday?

Tell her a joke on Friday.

• What do you call a brunette between two blondes?

An interpreter.

• What do you call a blonde between two brunettes?

Confused.

• How do you tell if a blonde is a good cook?

If the Pop-Tart is all in one piece.

• Why was the blonde so overjoyed after putting the jigsaw puzzle together in six weeks?

Because on the box it said: "Two to four years."

• How can you put a twinkle in a blonde's eye?

Shine a flashlight in her ear.

• Why don't blondes eat pickles?

Because they might get their heads stuck in the jar.

• What is the first thing a blonde does when she gets up in the morning?

She goes home.

• What do you call a basement full of blondes?

A whine cellar.

• What do you call it when a bug flies into a blonde's ear?

Space invasion.

• Why do blondes like the IRS?

Because they can spell it.

• What did the blonde name her pet zebra?

Spot.

But not all blondes are dumb. Like the beautiful blonde who was asked by her psychology professor if she thought she was a boy or a girl.

"I think I'm a boy," she responded.

"And why do you say that?" asked the professor.

"Because when I'm asked a dumb question, I give a dumb answer," she replied.

Case closed.

EQUAL TIME FOR "DUMB MEN" JOKES

It is inevitable that I will receive angry reaction to the last chapter, even though I wrote in the first paragraph that I don't like dumb blonde jokes and explained why. Some people won't read the first paragraph in their haste to get to the meat—the dumb blonde jokes. So I've included some dumb men to balance the book. They were sent to me by courier by someone named Judy Smythe after a column offended her.

Dumb Men Jokes (Strange, But True)

- Why are all dumb blonde jokes one liners?

  So men can understand them.

- What is the difference between government bonds and men?

  Government bonds eventually mature.

- What's a man's idea of helping with the housework?

  Lifting his legs so you can vacuum.

- What's the difference between a man and E.T.?

  E.T. phoned home.

- Why is psychoanalysis quicker for men than for women?

  When it's time to go back to his childhood, he's already there.

- What did God say after he created man?

  "I can do better than this."

- How do men define a fifty-fifty relationship?

  We cook/they eat; we clean/they dirty; we iron/they wrinkle.

- What's the best way to force a man to do sit-ups?

  Put the remote control between his toes.

- How do men exercise at the beach?

  By sucking in their stomachs every time they see a bikini.

- What does a man consider to be a seven-course meal?

  A hot dog and a six-pack.

- How are men like noodles?

  Both are always in hot

water, they have no taste, and they need dough.

- Why is it good that there are female astronauts?

When the crew gets lost at least the women will ask directions.

And there always is room for another definition or two when it comes to the relationship between the sexes:

- *Adam:* The first slave.
- *Automation:* Man's effort to make work so easy that women can do it all.
- *Bikini:* A bathing suit cut to see level.
- *Career girl:* One who gets a man's salary without marrying one.

- *Compromise:* Listening to your wife's opinion and deciding she's right.
- *Contented husband:* One who's on listening terms with his wife.
- *Discretion:* When a man is sure he's right but still asks his wife.
- *Gossip columnist:* One who writes others' wrongs.
- *Husband-hunting:* A sport in which the animal that gets caught has to buy the license.
- *Marriage:* A ceremony where the grocer acquires an account the florist once had.
- *Peroxide blonde:* A convertible top.
- *Stalemate:* A husband with one joke.

HALL OF FAME HOUSEKEEPER

Probably the two most exciting and mind-boggling purchases young people make in a lifetime are their first automobile and their first house. My daughter, Lisa, purchased her first car in Dublin several years ago. She and her husband, Keith, purchased their first house, in Macon, not long ago.

It's a very nice house and I'm probably as excited about their purchase as they are, maybe more. I don't have to make the payments.

I waited for three weeks before visiting their new domicile. Why so long? Simple. Even with my favorite daughter and favorite son-in-law, I needed an invitation, and it wasn't forthcoming until everything was in shipshape order.

Lisa is a great housekeeper. The girl actually loves to clean, mop, and scrub. She could take a bottle of cleaner, a couple of rags, a mop, and a Dirt Devil and clean up the mess in Florida left in the wake of Hurricane Andrew in about three days.

My initial visit to the new house was revealing from the outset. I parked in the backyard and walked to a side door, only to find two pairs of thongs standing at attention at the top step. I opened the door only to hear a blood-curdling scream from the lady of the house, "Take your shoes off before you enter!"

A pair of black tassel loafers joined the two pairs of thongs, and I was careful to line them up "just so." Even as I did so I couldn't help but wonder if somewhere way back there might have been some Japanese ancestors in my past. I mean, after all, both Keith and Lisa drive Japanese cars—she a Honda Accord and he a Toyota pickup. I made a mental note to have Allen Thomas and June Adams, Dublin's resident genealogists, check that out. But then I thought about the fella I know who paid out $1,000 to have his family tree traced only to fork over another $1,500 to the genealogist when he finished it to keep quiet about it.

I know Lisa is proud of her new house. But manicured (roofing) nails? Laminated door mats? Monogrammed dishrags? "Keith and Lisa" commode handles? I think that's a bit much, don't you?

Keith grilled steaks on my first visit. Delicious! After dinner Keith and I retired to the den to watch the Braves play the Reds. He was gracious enough to permit me to sit in his La-Z-Boy recliner, normally reserved for royalty—King Keith or Queen Lisa. Lisa was still outside Simonizing the barbecue grill and polishing the cooking fork.

Like I said, the girl is a great housekeeper. She joined us just after Terry Pendleton hit a home run.

Lisa is prone on occasion to light up a Virginia Slim. Her daddy will occasionally light up a Winston. In the den? No way! She escorted me to the designated smoking area, the front porch. "When in Rome, do as the Romans do." I understand that. I also understand that "When in Macon, do as Lisa does."

She went back inside before I did, and I couldn't help but notice through a spotless window that she was standing behind the La-Z-Boy headrest, holding a large magnifying glass in her left hand and a Dirt Devil vacuum in her right. Later, during a moment when Keith and I were alone and Lisa was dusting the bottom side of the telephone with a cashmere dusting cloth in the foyer, I asked Keith, "What was Lisa doing with the magnifying glass and Dirt Devil?"

"Oh, she was just making a dandruff check," he said routinely. "She does it to me all the time. And if she finds the evidence, out on the porch you go!"

Like I said, Lisa is a great housekeeper . . . but washing the dishes with Perrier water is a bit unusual.

A Hall of Fame Housekeeper

I was in Milledgeville on a rainy Friday night to watch Troup County High School (LaGrange) play Baldwin High. I was there because my oldest grandson, Jeremy Whaley, is on the Troup County team. A freshman who wears Number 20, he dressed out for his first game with no expectation of playing.

Also in attendance were his father, Joe, his mother, Cindy, his ten-year-old brother, Brett, Aunt Lisa, and Keith, one of his best buddies.

The rain started just before the opening kickoff and never stopped during the entire game. Torrent is the best word to describe it. Noah would have been wearing a raincoat and sporting an unbrella. His animals would have scurried to the nearest shelter on the ark. But not the Whaley clan. We were there for the duration. Two weeks later my wallet was still wet.

Now, for the big moment: Troup was leading 27–0 with 2:26 to play in the game. Several Troup substitutes sprinted on the field wearing unsoiled jerseys. And Number 20 was among them, weighing in at a strapping 140 pounds. Cindy spotted him first. Then she spotted a Baldwin player, Number 57, who weighed in at 295 and stood six feet, six inches. She made the inevitable comparison, bit her nails to just above her wrist, and offered up a wet prayer: "Oh, Lord! Please don't let him hurt my little boy!"

I said one, too, for the kid who just last year it seemed was sucking his thumb, talking in his sleep, and convinced that girls (cheerleaders) were a necessary evil.

All of us stood soaking wet at the fence surrounding the playing field. Baldwin had the ball. Number 20 was lined up at left defensive back. The Baldwin center snapped the ball to the quarterback, about six feet, one inch, and 185, who attempted to sweep right end. He didn't make it past the line of scrimmage. Enter Number 20 from Troup High, Jeremy. He charged, lowered his head, and plowed into the quarterback. The ball flew out of his arms and Troup recovered. Luckily, so did Jeremy. He had made his first tackle.

Was I proud? Shoot, I reckon! Rain? What rain? It was a perfect night. Cindy cheered. Joe cheered. Brett cheered. Lisa went into hysterics. Keith grinned a broad, proud smile. Granddaddy Bo dang near jumped the fence.

Then Lisa the housekeeper did her thing. Get the picture now: Her nephew had just moments before made his first tackle, causing the Baldwin quarterback to fumble and Troup recovered. Jeremy's teammates were congratulating him, patting him on the head and butt, and calling him by name. The cheerleaders were jumping up and down. The moment was as big for Jeremy as was the closing on her new house for his Aunt Lisa.

Above the crowd noise I heard Lisa's voice as she yelled to the entire Whaley clan, all of whom would return to her house in Macon to spend the night: "Remember, now! Everybody take your shoes off when we get to my house! And smoking *only* on the porch!"

Joe, who occasionally lights up a Vantage, turned to me and said, "I can tell you that I'm very familiar with that porch, Dad."

SKIPPY AND SUPERWOMEN

I 've long been a Skippy Lawson fan. Ten years ago I labeled her the "Erma Bombeck of the South."

I found one of her columns recently while rummaging through a box of columns I'd saved. Here it is:

I Hate Superwomen

I've given up reading ladies' homemaking magazines. They give me an inferiority complex.

What bothers me is the inevitable article about the Homemaker of the Year. She's attractive, with seven smiling children and a proud-looking husband. There's a picture of the happy family, in front of their home.

The children are in front, smiling like angels. Not one is pinching, kicking, stepping on the toes of, or otherwise harassing the one next to him. Not one is sticking his tongue out or making faces. Not one is wiggling, squirming, pulling at his collar, or scratching anywhere.

No one's children behave long enough for that kind of picture. At least one would backslide.

Behind the children are the parents. The Homemaker of the Year has shiny, well-kept hair. The article tells you she does it herself, saving the money she would spend at the beauty parlor for family outings.

Her dress is tailored perfectly. So are her children's clothes. The article tells you she makes all of her family's clothes— including her husband's shirts and ties. Also the sheets, towels, afghans, bedspreads, pillow cases, curtains, and drapes— in her spare time.

Her husband is smiling fondly, wearing a shirt and tie she made for him.

Down in the lefthand corner is the family dog. He has a shiny, silken coat. He's not scratching fleas or licking anywhere and hasn't just been running through a field of beggar lice or cockleburs. He's not gnawing on the newspaper. The article tells you that each day the Homemaker of the Year brushes and combs the dog and takes him to obedience school—in her spare time.

She loves to cook. Photos show her in the kitchen, happily stirring whatever is in the pot. Her children aren't hanging around yelling, "But I'm hungry *now!*" Instead, the little darlings are setting the table. And they are not fighting over who will put out the forks and who will put out the napkins. It seems her children never fight. She has taught them to share and compromise—in her spare time.

The house is immaculate. No handprints around the light switches. The houseplants are green and thriving. No drooping stems or fallen leaves with mysterious brown spots. Through the window flowers can be seen blooming in the garden. She loves to garden and arranges flowers she has grown—in her spare time.

The yard is neat and clean. She cuts the grass and trims the shrubbery. Money that would have been paid to a yardman goes into the kitty for family outings.

Not one tree has two-by-fours nailed to it. There are no odd-looking structures, forts, clubhouses, or treehouses, visible anywhere in the yard. No tricycles, bicycles, or toys clutter the driveway. They are kept in the shelter behind the garage that she built to house them—in her spare time.

She holds down a full-time executive position with a large advertising firm and does volunteer work at the hospital. She teaches a Sunday school class, is president of the garden club, a den mother, chairman of the PTO fund-raising committee, plays the organ at Sunday morning church services, and is the chief organizer of the county humane society. And she plants landscapes—in her spare time.

What's her secret? (Here comes the part that really makes me sick.) She says: "I make sure I get plenty of rest."

CAUTION: COMPLIMENT WITH CARE

I went to one of my favorite restaurants in Middle Georgia, Cedar Lane Supper Club in McRae, with my favorite girl. I enjoyed my favorite beef cut, prime rib, and my favorite salad bar. But one dimension was missing—my favorite waitress, Ramona.

"Where's Ramona?" I asked the owner, Aubrey Stone.

"She's not here tonight," he said. "She's kinda down in the dumps."

"What's wrong?"

"She quit smoking three weeks ago and—"

"Why would that put her in the dumps? She ought to be proud of herself."

"Well, it's like this," Aubrey said. "One of my regular customers came in last week. Ramona's his favorite waitress, too. Like everybody else, he picks at her a lot. He said she appeared to have put on a few pounds around the middle and—"

"And that upset her?"

"Did it ever! She ain't had a bite to eat since."

"You tell that pretty girl not to worry about it," I suggested. "Tell her for me that in my opinion she is the best-looking twenty-three-year-old fat girl in Telfair County."

I like to toss compliments around. Next time I see Ramona, I know she'll be glad to see me. Flattery will get the job done every time . . . or will it? I may find out.

It has been said that "flattery will get you everywhere." Also that "flattery will get you nowhere." But I'm thinking that "flattery can also get you a pair of black eyes and a busted nose," like in this classic about a good ole boy, Roscoe, and his girlfriend, Susie Mae:

Roscoe was crazy about Susie Mae. He was plum moon-eyed about her. But he wasn't making any progress with his courtship of Susie Mae. So, he sought advice from the Don Juan of the county, Reggie.

"Reggie," Roscoe said, "You always seem to make out real good with the girls, but I ain't making no progress with Susie Mae. Can ya help me?"

"Do you ever compliment her? All girls love to be complimented," Reggie said.

"Whadda' ya' mean, compliment her?"

"You just pick out one of her outstanding features and compliment her on it. You know, brag on her?"

"Well, I ain't never done it, but I'll try if you think it'll help," Roscoe promised.

Several days later Reggie saw Roscoe pull his pickup into the gas station and get out. He had two black eyes and a broken nose.

"What happened?" Reggie asked. "You run into a bulldozer or something?"

"Naw, nothin' like that," Roscoe allowed. "But it's your fault."

"My fault? How do you figure that?" Reggie asked, frowning.

"Well, I tried what you said with Susie Mae, and she dang near killed me."

"What happened?"

"Me and her went to the Saturday night dance. Then we got some hamburgers and came back to her house. You know how much Susie Mae likes to eat," Roscoe said. "It was a real hot night so we set in the swing on the front porch. They was a full moon and it was a real pretty night; so I done what you said."

"What's that?" Reggie asked.

"I gave her one o' them compliments like you told me to do and she dropped her hamburger and hit me in the face with her fists."

"What did you say to her?"

"I looked right in them pretty blue eyes and said "Susie Mae, 'for a big ole fat girl you shore don't sweat much.'"

I'LL FALL IN LOVE AT THE DROP OF A PACIFIER

I have been characterized by some women as a male chauvinist pig, a female-bashing, womanizing redneck. Not true.

I am a softhearted, female-admiring, good ole southern boy and cherish my female friends.

I like women, love ladies, and adore girls—especially little girls. And I fall in love a lot. I'll fall in love at the drop of a pacifier or the swish of a ponytail.

Over the past ten years I've fallen in love many times and have a love affair going now. She just turned ten a few days ago, and she's a living doll. Her name is Laura. What a pretty name for a pretty girl. I'm going to tell you about Laura in the next chapter, but for now I'm going to reveal the details of my relationships with the other seven.

• *Misty:* I fell in love with Misty in 1983. She was seven and the mascot of my morning radio show. I was fifty-six. I'd marry her, but her mama won't let me. But then, even if I should marry Misty I wouldn't know whether to take her on a honeymoon, send her to camp, or burp her.

In the past ten years I've attended Misty's dance concerts, "Nutcracker" performances, enjoyed Dairy Queen blizzards with her, taught her how to drive (and parallel park), exchanged Christmas and birthday gifts with her, and dined with her at the country club when she was twelve. It was a special evening, and I was proud to present her with her first corsage.

Misty was radiant. I was proud.

But Misty grew up on me. I watched the transformation as she changed from a cute little girl to the beautiful young lady she is today at seventeen. I'm fortunate. Misty has remained a friend, a good friend.

I love her. She's special to

me, and always will be. She knows it.

• *Gina Dee:* Gina Dee came into my life at the ripe old age of nine. When she turned twelve, I had a special evening with her planned. With her parents' permission, we were to go to the country club for dinner. But on the day before our date Gina Dee broke her arm.

I accused her of breaking her arm on purpose to keep from having to be seen with me in public. She denied it. I visited her in the hospital, and she showed me a prescription that her doctor had written for her. It read thusly:

"Under no circumstances should you go out to dinner with Bo Whaley." (With unlimited refills.)

Typical of a fourteen-year-old, Gina Dee went against her doctor's orders two years later; and we went to a fine restaurant, Annabelle's, for dinner on her fourteenth birthday. She was beautiful. I was the most envied sixty-two-year-old there. It was a great evening.

But, like Misty, Gina Dee grew up on me and discovered boys and cars. She became even prettier, got her driver's license and her car at age sixteen. I called her a few months later. Naturally, she wasn't home. I talked briefly with her mother, Susan, who's as pretty as Gina Dee.

"I have no idea where she is, Bo," Susan said. "I haven't seen or heard from her since she got her driver's license."

Gina Dee promised to take me for a ride in her new car. As of this writing I haven't heard from her. I'm waiting.

• *Allison:* I fell hard for Allison when she was thirteen, and I was a spry and silly sixty-one. If you knew Allison, you'd know why. Pretty, very sweet, and not stingy with her hugs.

Allison dealt me a severe blow to the heart when she was fourteen. I still haven't completely recovered.

It happened on a chartered bus as we sat together, in the first seat behind the driver, on the way back home from a University of Georgia football game. I don't remember who won. Who cares? I was with Allison.

I guess it must have been the uniform. Girls go for uniforms of any kind and the bus driver's obviously impressed Allison.

When we left Athens, Georgia, Allison was mine—all mine. When we got off the bus in Dublin, Bubba had moved in and I was out in the cold.

I went straight home and took my old World War II uniform out of mothballs. Too little, and C&H Bus Lines wasn't hiring. The Salvation Army turned down my application.

Allison was Dublin High School's Homecoming Queen in 1992. I called the shot a week before she was crowned, sending her a premature letter of congratulations. Was I proud? You bet I was.

While Bubba, in uniform, stole Allison from me, every cloud has a silver lining. Allison has a sister, Mandy.

● *Mandy:* It began with Mandy when she was seven, and fifty-five years ain't really that big an age gap. I proceeded slowly and cautiously. Then, at age eight, the smiles and hugs began to come regularly. Both are irresistible. Now, Mandy's fourteen. They're still coming. I look forward to them.

I really think it was the smile that did it. I could no more resist it than a bear can resist honey. One of Mandy's smiles can turn on a burned-out light bulb.

Like the others, Mandy's growing away from me; but I'll never let her get away completely. She has something of mine that is vital to me. She has a piece of my heart, a *big* piece. Do I love her? Hah! Is water wet?

● *Lori:* I was no doubt attracted to Lori because of her maturity. She was an "older" fourteen when I made my pitch.

I crashed Lori's fifteenth birthday dinner at the Elks Club. She was with her mother and father, but something was missing. There were no cake and no candles.

I improvised, hastening to locate a cupcake and candles at an all-night supermarket. Also, I pilfered a camera from the *Courier Herald*, my newspaper.

The cupcake, with lighted candle, was presented and I followed with a capital crime by murdering "Happy Birthday" in song. Then I took pictures, nearly as many as she's had taken in recent weeks as the 1992 Saint Patrick's Festival Queen.

True to form, Lori was sweet and patient. She abided the antics of an old man making a fool of himself over a beautiful girl.

Lori's birthday dinner is a good memory. So is Lori.

• *Kellye:* Kellye is the "senior citizen" of my pacifier harem. She's an old and wrinkled nineteen, but gorgeous.

Kellye is special. She understands me, and that's no easy task. She tolerates me. And I think she likes me. I hope so.

Kellye is also tolerant. She has to be. She works for me. She typed the manuscript that finally became this book. (There is a special acknowledgment from me recognizing Kellye's contribution in the front of the book.)

Cute? Neat? Smart? Efficient? Fun? All these adjectives apply to Kellye.

Best of all, her parents trust me. I like that.

As of this writing I have two more on hold, Jessica, eight, and Kaylie, nine. Both are future queens and, while they may not know it yet, they are Bo Whaley sweethearts.

I have a theory about becoming friends with little girls. You don't push them. You don't rush them. Like feeding a bird, you offer your friendship gently in one hand and offer it slowly, like a summer sunrise or cane syrup oozing from a bottle in midwinter. If you're lucky, they'll accept it and return it. I'll tell you about one, Laura Little, who did, if you'll just turn to the next chapter.

LAURA

It all started when Laura Little was six and beautiful. She's now ten and beautiful, and a new friend.

I first spotted Laura in the back booth at Ma Hawkins Restaurant. She was there with her mother, Lynn, to see her grandmother, Carolyne Garner. One look at Lynn and it's easy to see how Laura came about her beauty.

First, there was eye contact between Laura and me. Actually, she caught me staring. She fashioned a faint smile. I didn't push her, but I knew that somehow, someday, Laura would be my friend. Admittedly, I would work through her grandmother who has been a good friend for fifteen years. I kept up with Laura through her.

For two years the eye contact, polite smiles, and cautious greetings continued. Then, one afternoon it happened. Laura made the move I'd hoped she'd make. She approached me at a front table in Ma Hawkins.

"Mr. Bo," she said, "would you like to see some new clothes I've made for my doll?"

My answer, naturally, was in the affirmative.

"Sure. I'd love to see them."

Laura scampered to the back booth. Nine-year-olds have a tendency to scamper, while old men have a tendency to creep.

She returned with the doll clothes in hand. I was impressed. I really was impressed. She showed me several outfits and allowed as how she loved to sew. She should. She's good at it.

The door had been opened. Laura had come to me after three years. I liked that. In the weeks that followed the smiles became brighter, the conversations more open and longer, and we shared a more relaxed feeling when in each other's presence.

While we "Howdy" now on a regular basis, we ain't hugged yet. But then, doesn't every man long for something to look forward to?

Later I was given a message from Laura by her grandmother, Carolyne.

"There's a science fair being held at the Dublin Mall next

weekend, on Friday and Saturday," Carolyne told me. "Laura has a project entered and would like for you to come and see it."

I was out of the state on Friday but drove home Saturday and headed straight for the mall. Laura wasn't there, but her project was—adorned with a blue ribbon. First place! I wasn't surprised. Laura is accustomed to blue ribbons and first place. At age ten she has lots of both, with many years to go.

The week following the science fair I saw Laura in Ma Hawkins. I congratulated her. She smiled. That was enough. It was time for me to make my move.

I figured that after four years the time was right. I asked her mother if I might visit with Laura in their home, talk with her, and maybe take a few pictures. She, along with Laura, consented and I drove up to her home.

Saturday Morning with Laura

It was a pretty morning. I had intended to take a few pictures, visit for a short time, and leave. Not so. I took a few pictures, Laura gave me a tour of her sewing room, her bedroom, and her trophy room. I stayed for the better part of an hour.

First, I watched her sew on her sewing machine. I was impressed. She's no amateur with needle and thread. She posed for a picture.

Next, she escorted me to her very own room and showed me her mountain of stuffed animals. Shouldn't every pretty little girl have a bunch of stuffed animals? I think so. She posed for a picture.

Next, she explained the many achievement certificates and plaques that covered her wall—like Physical Education, History, Handwriting, Science, Art, Student of the Week at Bleckley Elementary where she is a fourth grade student, and more, many more. She posed for a picture.

We moved from her room to the living room for a little girl-boy (old man) talk. But we did it right. We were appropriately chaperoned by her mother, Lynn, who watched me like a mother hawk from her vantage point in a rocker about fifteen feet away. Did I say we were chaperoned? Boy! Were we ever! Lynn had even arranged for a backup. She brought in her sister from Conyers, just in case. Laura posed for a picture.

In talking with Laura I learned that her hobbies are sewing, skating, swimming in the Allentown pool, and reading. Her favorite author is Ann M. Martin, and she reads two books a month. Her favorite subjects are spelling and math.

She participated in Exploration–1992, an acting workshop at Georgia College, and finished in the top 20 percent. She has been selected as one of a number of students to go on a school trip to Savannah. Her best friends? She answered that promptly and easily.

"Lauren Ledbetter and Kinsey Wade," she said.

Then, we got into the good stuff like future plans for college, a possible vocation, goals, and boyfriends!

"I don't suppose you've given much thought at this point to college and—" I started.

Laura began rattling off comments like a machine gun.

"Oh, yes! I'm going to go to college for four years, two at Middle Georgia and then two at Emory. Then, I'm going to be a magazine model and be in the Miss USA Pageant and after that get married and have three children, two girls and a boy, and—"

"What was that?" yelled Lynn, coming up out of her chair like a rocket.

"Right, two girls and a boy," Laura repeated. (Lynn sat back down.)

"Want to see a picture of my boyfriend?" she asked.

"Uh . . . sure. Yeah, I'd like to see it," I stammered.

"And so would I!" Lynn chimed in.

Laura scampered off again and returned with her school yearbook. She turned the pages and then stopped to point to a neat young man in her class. (By this time Lynn was looking over my shoulder.)

"He's a nice looking boy, Laura," I said.

"Thanks," she said with a smile. "He's nice, too."

"I'll bet he is."

I was having fun. I hated to leave, but the time had come.

Mamas and little girls have things to do on Saturday mornings . . .

I was walking to my car. Laura and her mother stood on the back porch. I turned and spoke to Lynn:

"I have just one more question," I said.

"Sure, what's that?"

"Can I take Laura home with me?"

I don't have to tell you her answer.

You see, I used to have a Misty, Gina Dee, Allison, Mandy, Lori, Jessica, Kaylie, and Kellye; but Laura did the same thing they're doing to me. She grew up. I guess I'm just trying to find her again.

Her name is Lisa. She, like all the others, is sweet and beautiful. If you happen to see her, tell her I love her and that while I realize full well that nobody can take her place, I refuse to give up. In fact, I found another at the country club yesterday. Her name is Bliss. A little doll. She won't talk to me yet, but I'm working on it. Actually, we barely made eye contact before she buried her face in her hands on the back of a chair. Oh, by the way—Bliss is three.

PART FIVE

ANECDOTES AND BRAIN TWISTERS

I'm convinced that everybody should have a hobby. I've had one since childhood: I collect joke books, jokes, and trivia. When I hear a new joke or tidbit of trivia, I immediately make a note of it. On a good day my pockets overflow with notes.

Show me a man without a sense of humor, and I'll show you an empty man. I can think of nothing healthier than a good clean belly laugh. I don't even bother to take out pencil and paper for the dirty jokes, although they are now in abundance. If you don't think so, flip on your television set.

I've included several jokes and trivia stories that are among my recent favorites. Of course, there are many more that I had no room for. Like these:

• A man and his wife had been married for forty years. They were having dinner on their anniversary when she said to him, "Harry, do you realize that we have been married for forty years, and you haven't once told me you loved me since our wedding night?'

Harry wiped his mouth with his napkin, placed it gently on the table, looked his wife right in the eye, and said, "Well, Mildred, if I ever change my mind, I'll let you know."

• The boy and girl had been dating for two years. He was extremely ugly but had a great job as a traveling salesman working out of town Monday through Friday. She was breathtakingly beautiful but from a poor family, and she was getting impatient.

"Tom, we have been seeing each other for two years now, and you have given not the slightest indication of your intentions regarding marriage," she said one night after dinner.

"Well, Jean, it's like this: You are so beautiful, and I am so ugly, I just don't think it would be fair to you for me to ask you to marry me," he explained in all seriousness.

"Oh, that's all right!" she exclaimed excitedly. "I've thought about that a lot and—"

"You have? Well, what do you think?"

"Well, the way I figure it is this," she said. "You see, Tom, you'll be gone most of the time . . ."

• At a Las Vegas gambler's funeral, the preacher asserted, "Remember this, Spike is not dead, he only sleeps."

Several of his gambling friends who were in attendance sat in a front row pew in the chapel. One elbowed the one next to him and whispered, "I got $100 that says he's dead."

A RETORT IS MORE THAN JUST A REPLY

One night recently I reached for the *Reader's Digest* and flipped through it in search of a short story. I found it on page 117, "The Clever Retort."

Retort is defined thusly: "To turn an insult back upon the person from which it came."

The story focused on the 1988 debate between vice-presidential candidates Lloyd Bentsen and Dan Quayle. It related how much more fun it would have been if Quayle had responded with a brilliant comeback to Bentsen's insulting quip, "Senator, you're no Jack Kennedy." Quayle's response, "That was really uncalled for, Senator," was too tame. He needed a combination of wit and wisdom—a clever line.

Based on what we've learned about the dark side of Jack Kennedy's character—his sexual antics, his cruel use of women—maybe Quayle didn't need to respond wittily upon being told he was no Jack Kennedy. Maybe all he needed to say was, "Thank you."

A Few Classic Retorts

• Sir Winston Churchill was a master of the retort. Like his reply to Bessie Braddock, a member of Parliament, who bellowed at him during a dinner party, "Mr. Churchill, you're drunk!" to which Churchill replied, "And you, madam, are ugly. But in the morning I shall be sober."

On another occasion an English lady approached Churchill after he had delivered a speech while sporting a mustache. "Sir, I neither care for your mustache nor your politics."

"It is highly unlikely, madam, that you shall ever come in contact with either," replied Churchill.

• My favorite Churchill retort is this one: Bernard Shaw sent Churchill two tickets to the opening night of one of his plays, along with a note: "One for yourself and one for a friend—if you have one."

Churchill returned the tickets with this note: "Unable to attend opening night performance but would appreciate two tickets for the second-night performance—if there is one."

• What many consider the world's wittiest retort is attributed to John Wilkes, eighteenth-century British journalist and politician.

When Lord Sandwich offered the opinion that Wilkes would die "either of the pox or on the gallows," Wilkes shot back, "That will depend on whether I embrace your lordship's mistress or your lordship's principles."

• The beauty of the clever retort is that the aggressor sets himself or herself up to be the victim. Here's a classic example:

Noel Coward once encountered Edna Ferber, who was wearing a tailored suit. "You look almost like a man," said Coward.

"So do you," said Ferber.

• A touch of the absurd can be devastating in the right hands. Case in point:

An English duke, annoyed by the slow service and/or the lack of proper recognition at his London club, summoned a new waiter to his table and said gruffly, "Young man, do you know who I am?"

The waiter replied, coolly, "No, sir, I don't. But I shall make inquiries and inform you directly."

• It has been reported that on one occasion Dorothy Parker and Clare Booth Luce approached a doorway at the same time. Luce stepped aside and said pompously, "Age before beauty," to which Parker replied as she swept past her and through the door, "Pearls before swine."

• One of the cleverest retorts I've ever heard or read concerns this exchange between a waitress and a haughty female customer who was always very demanding and curt:

"Would you answer me this, young lady?" she said to the waitress. "Why is it that I never receive the service I deserve from the employees in this establishment?"

"Quite possible, madam," replied the waitress, "it is because we are too polite."

CLASSROOM HUMOR

I guess we don't normally think of education as being humorous. There are, however some classic humorous stories that have come from the classroom.

I have always enjoyed educational humor and three of my most delightful years were spent as a teacher at Dublin High School. That's when I began collecting classroom humor. Here are some of my favorites.

- How come a fourteen-year-old boy can unwrap a candy bar while holding a sweater, a basketball, and two books, yet he can't put a garbage can cover on straight with two hands?

- Father of a high-schooler in an affluent suburb asked, "Well, what did you learn today?"

The high-schooler replied, "I learned that if I don't start getting to school fifteen minutes earlier, I won't get a place to park."

- Sunday school teacher: "Who defeated the Philistines?"

Student: "I don't know. I don't keep track of the minor leagues."

- Third-grade teacher to her class: "Does anyone know why a bear sleeps in his cave during winter?"

Eight-year-old Susan waved her hand excitedly. "I think I know!"

"And what's your answer, Susan?" asked the teacher.

"Because there's no one brave enough to go in there and wake him up," Susan explained.

- "What parable," a Sunday school teacher asked a fourth-grade student, "do you like best?"

"The one," replied the student, "about the multitude that loafs and fishes."

- A teacher was explaining the wonders science has discovered about the universe. "Just think," she exclaimed, "light comes all the way from the sun at a speed of 186,000 miles per second. Isn't that almost unbelievable?"

"Aw, I dunno," reported one unimpressed youngster. "After all, it's downhill all the way."

• Rosalie was in her first semester in college when her mother received a special delivery letter from her:

"Dear Mother: Please send me $75 for a new dress right away. I've had six dates with Johnny and have worn each of the dresses I brought with me. I have another date next Monday night and must have another dress right away."

Her mother replied via Western Union: "Get another boyfriend and start over."

• The rural school teacher in Michigan, on the first real cold spell of winter, cautioned her pupils about the dangers of playing on ice-covered ponds and streams. She admonished, "Now, students, you must be sure the ice is safe. I had a little brother, only eight years old. One day he went skating on the lake near here with his new skates. He broke through the thin ice and drowned."

After a period of silence, a freckle-faced boy in the back of the room raised his hand and asked eagerly, "Where's his skates?"

• Teacher: "Now, spell straight."

Small Pupil: "S-T-R-A-I-G-H-T."

Teacher: "Correct. Now, what does it mean?"

Small Pupil: "Without water."

• The college president was disciplining an unruly freshman. "I am told," he said, "that you have a barrel of beer in your dormitory room."

"Doctor's orders, sir," the freshman replied. "He said if I drank a lot of beer I'd get my strength back."

"Hmmmm . . . and did you?"

"Absolutely! When that barrel came in, I could hardly budge it; and now I can roll it all around the room!"

A FEW BITS AND PIECES

I attended a nice party at a friend's clubhouse. As the evening wore on, somebody kept turning the volume up on the jukebox until it reached the point of being almost unbearable. Many of the guests sought refuge outside on the porch.

Near midnight, one guest came out with a drink in hand, and a friend said to him, "What's the matter, Luke? The music too loud for you, too?"

"Too loud? Heck, no. I'm just taking a little break. And I'll tell you this. I ain't never heard a bad band or seen an ugly woman after eleven o'clock."

At a dinner party a female attorney found herself seated next to a male doctor, and they got to discussing the nuisance of constantly being approached for free professional advice during social situations.

"I never know how to handle it gracefully," she admitted. "Got any advice?"

"Well, I don't know if this will work for you," said the doctor, "but I stop them cold with one word."

"What's that?" the attorney asked.

"Undress."

I enjoyed a great visit with two of my favorite people, Pete and Paula Raymer, in the backyard seated by the pool. No television, just good conversation.

Their daughter, Graham, joined us and told me this story.

A girl had met the man of her dreams—a tall, dark, and handsome fella with a great appetite. He was also very rural, a man of the woods, and an avid hunter and fisherman. She was somewhat sophisticated and a great cook.

She invited her Romeo over for dinner and prepared her specialty—chicken, wine, mushrooms, Vidalia onions, tomatoes, and artichoke hearts. She placed the concoction in a Crock Pot and cooked it for hours until it was just right.

Later, when she proudly placed her handiwork before her man, he began eating heartily. And he was very complimentary. As he progressed, he held an artichoke heart on a fork and asked, "And what is this?"

"That's an artichoke heart," she said with beaming anticipation. "Do you like it?"

"Oh, yes!" he said. "I don't usually eat organs like liver, kidneys, and gizzards, but this heart is delicious!"

It was the man's first visit to an eminent urologist, and the doctor was taking down his medical history. "And whom have you consulted about your condition before coming to me?" asked the great doctor.

"Only the pharmacist at Brown's Drug Store," the man replied rather sheepishly.

The doctor made no effort to conceal his contempt for the sort of advice available from those who dispensed medical advice without a license to do so. "Idiots like that only aggravate most conditions," he grumbled. "And what absurd recommendations did that moron come up with?"

"He told me to come and see you."

There was considerable jealousy surrounding a Dr. Atkinson who had the luxury of a telephone in his Bentley.

A fellow plastic surgeon had a telephone installed in his Porsche. The first call he placed was to Dr. Atkinson.

"George," he said, "I just want you to know that you're not the only doctor in Los Angeles who can afford a telephone in his car."

"Hang on a second, would you, Phil?" interrupted Atkinson. "I've got another call on my other phone."

"Which side is best to lie on, Doctor?" asked the lawyer at a cocktail party, seeking some free medical advice.

"The side that pays you the retainer," the doctor answered savagely.

DOCTORS AND LAWYERS ARE GOOD TARGETS

It doesn't take long for a new joke to make the rounds. Take President George Bush's unfortunate incident when he fell out of his chair and regurgitated while attending a dinner with Japanese officials. It was a case of the flu, President Bush explained, but one gag writer wrote otherwise: "Mrs. Bush stood, took one look at her husband, and assured those in attendance that 'George is all right. He's just doing his Ted Kennedy imitation.'"

I'm sure the gag writer was pecking the gag out on his typewriter before Mr. Bush was up off the floor and seated again. There is nothing sacred to gag writers, and elected officials are among their favorite targets, the more highly placed the better. Other targets are doctors and lawyers. Let's look at a few:

- A man walked into a psychiatrist's office in Los Angeles. He had a strip of breakfast bacon dangling from his right ear, a green olive in his right nostril, and a black one in his left. The receptionist ushered him in to see the psychiatrist quickly.

"What can I do for you?" asked the psychiatrist.

"I want to speak to you about my brother—you see, he's got this problem . . ."

- Everybody is concerned about crime today. I'll never forget the time when a guy wearing a mask took all my money. I was in surgery at the time.

- A doctor was asked if he could admit to any mistakes. He said, "Yes, I once cured a multimillionaire in only three visits."

- A general practitioner was asked the difference between a specialist and a regular M.D.

"The specialist has a bigger boat," he explained.

- After informing the doctor that there was nothing wrong with his car, the mechanic handed him a bill for fifty dollars.

"What? If there's nothing

wrong with it, how come you're charging me fifty dollars?" the doctor screamed.

"Well, it's like this, Doc," the mechanic said, "you charged me fifty dollars for a visit last week, and I didn't have anything wrong either."

• "Before I take this case," the counselor said, "you'll have to give me a thousand dollars."

George agreed: "All right, here's your thousand."

The lawyer thanked him and said, "This entitles you to two questions."

George screamed, "What? A thousand bucks for two questions? Isn't that awfully high?"

"Yes, I suppose it is," said the attorney. "Now then, what's your second question?"

• The defendant was asked by the judge, "Now then, tell me, Mr. Dunwoody, can you walk?"

"Well, Judge, it's like this. My doctor says I can walk, but my lawyer says I can't," Dunwoody explained.

• The two attorneys were talking over lunch.

"As soon as I realized it was a crooked deal I got out of it," said one.

"Oh, yeah? How much?"

• One poor fellow consulted a lawyer to find out if he needed legal advice. He said no and sent him a bill for $300. Two days later he was at a party and met another lawyer. He explained that all he did was ask the first lawyer if he needed legal advice and he sent him a bill for $300 for legal advice. "Can he do that?"

"Yes," said the second lawyer.

The next morning the second lawyer sent him a bill for $300 for legal advice.

GOOD NEWS, BAD NEWS

R ev. Lamar Holley of Dublin First Baptist Church called me on a Saturday afternoon. His voice was vibrating with desperation.

"Bo, I need a favor," he said.

"You've got it," I replied. "What can I do for you?"

"Well, it's like this: I'm putting the finishing touches on my sermon for tomorrow and I desperately need two good news/bad news jokes. Can you help me?" he asked.

"I think so. I'll just type 'em up and drop them in your mailbox at the church," I said.

Here are the two I gave him, and he used both:

• The doctor walked into his patient's hospital room, 216, and said to the occupant, "George, I'm afraid I have both good news and bad news for you. Which do you want to hear first?"

"Let me have the bad news, Doc."

"All right. I have just finished studying your X-rays and both your feet have to be amputated in the morning," the doctor said.

"And he good news?" George quizzed.

"The fella in Room 214 wants to buy your shoes."

• A woman came home from an all-day shopping spree and was told by her neighbor that a man called and left a message for her, regarding her regularly unemployed son. "He left his number and wants you to call him right away. He just said he works 'downtown' and needs to talk to you."

The woman called the number, the police department, and was pleased when a Lieutenant Mitchell said, "Your son opened a convenience store just after lunch today and—"

"Oh, that's good news!" the woman shouted enthusiastically.

"Would you like the bad news?" asked the lieutenant.

"Yes, please!"

"It wasn't your son's store."

*　　*　　*

Here are a few others that I could have given the good reverend:

- "Well, I've got good news and bad news for you," the doctor told his patient. "The bad news is that you only have twenty-four hours to live."

"So, what's the good news?" the patient asked.

"I could have told you yesterday," the doctor replied.

- After completing his examination of a soon-to-be-married, very nervous young man, the doctor told him that he had both good and bad news to report to him. "John, your fiancèe has a very bad venereal disease."

"And the good news?"

"She didn't catch it from you!"

- These days everybody wants a second opinion—Like the lady who had been seeing a psychiatrist for years and decided one day she'd had enough of it.

"Doctor," she announced when she walked into his office, "I've been seeing you every Thursday for five years now. I don't feel any better. What's the story? Give it to me straight. What's wrong with me?"

"OK. I'll tell you: you're crazy," replied the doctor matter-of-factly.

"Now wait just a minute," protested the woman, "I want a second opinion."

"Fine," said the doctor. "You're ugly, too."

- Patient: "Doctor, nobody ever listens to me."

Psychiatrist: "Who's next?"

RESTAURANT TALK

Washington Pie was the featured dessert. He ordered a slice, and when the waiter brought it, it was white and fluffy with red cherries all over the top. The pie was out of this world as to real good taste. It was delicious.

Some few weeks later the fellow went back to the same restaurant. He was pleased to see Washington Pie on the menu. He ordered it again. The waiter left and returned soon with a generous slice of rich chocolate pie. The customer enjoyed it but was somewhat surprised at the change.

He told the waiter he had expected to get the pretty white pie with cherries on top and asked him what had happened. The waiter's reply was, "Oh, we have Washington Pie nearly every day at this restaurant. Some days it is George, and some days it is Booker T."

• Restaurant prices have reached a point where a fellow from a small South Georgia town, experimenting at a highly touted new restaurant in Atlanta, told the waiter, "I'm not very hungry, so I think I'll try your ten-dollar dinner."

"Very good," noted the waiter. "Will you have your coffee black or with cream?"

"I'll decide that when I've finished my dinner," said the South Georgian.

"Pardon me, sir," corrected the waiter. "Coffee *is* our ten-dollar dinner."

• A customer had been trying in vain to get some service in a crowded midtown restaurant one lunchtime. Finally, he beseeched the majordomo and asked, "Could you change my table, please?"

"Certainly, sir. Do you have a preference?"

"Yes, I'd appreciate one near a waiter."

• A restaurant proprietor told his wife happily, "Well, I finally found out today what's been happening to all those oysters we've been missing in the kitchen. That fool new cook has been putting them in the oyster stew."

• During the Saturday night rush hour at a popular Long Island inn, one of the parking attendants was summoned to help check hats and coats in the jammed-up cloakroom. In his first quarter of an hour he dented over nine overcoats.

• One of my favorite stories regarding restaurants and dining concerns a good friend, now deceased, who lived in Candler County. I'll just call him Joe. Although I heard the story repeated many times, I doubt its validity. But I like it anyway.

The story goes that several men from Candler County were invited to attend a farm machinery exposition in Chicago. Joe was among them. The men were entertained royally.

On the final night of their five-night stay, they were treated to dinner at a fashionable restaurant. The steaks were fabulous, mouth watering. Then, the waiter came to their table and asked, "Would anyone care for dessert?"

Joe, not wanting to miss a thing, said, "Yeah, I believe I will."

"Very good, sir," said the waiter. "And what would you like?"

"Pie," Joe said.

"And what kind of pie, sir?" asked the waiter.

"What kind? Sweet potato pie! What the heck do you think pie is made of?"

MORE GRIN AND SHARE IT

I've never made a big deal out of birthdays. After all, everybody has one, and they come around annually. Oh, I can understand the enthusiasm that birthdays bring to kids; but for those of us who belong to the Geritol and bifocal crowd, birthdays are really nothing more than another notch in the handle of life's six-gun.

There are those, however, who insist on remembering the older folks with birthday cards and gifts. On my birthday I received some of both, including four new joke books.

Joke books provide an entertaining diversion, a chance to get away from the dispenser of bad news—television. I'm really enjoying the four new books and here's why, some of the gags and giggles that caught my fancy when reviewing them.

● "Excuse me, but could you spare five dollars to help bury a rap musician?"

"Here's ten. Bury two of 'em."

● The wealthy elderly lady was disgusted by the sight of the ragged, unkempt hobo who asked her for a handout.

"You filthy man," she said. "Don't you even own a handkerchief?"

"Yeah, I do, lady," the hobo replied, "but I don't like loaning it out."

● Wife to husband: "Have you looked in our cupboards lately? There's eighteen bottles of whiskey and two loaves of bread."

Husband: "Oh, yeah? What are you gonna do with all that bread?"

● "She says with her new haircut she doesn't look like an old lady anymore. What do you think?"

"She's right. She now looks like an old man."

● Priest to caddie (after shooting a 66 on the front nine): "I wonder if it would help my golf score if I prayed before I teed off on the back nine?"

Caddie: "Only if you keep your head down, Father."

● Sunday school teacher: "Miss Johnson, could you tell the rest of our Sunday school class the name of the first man?"

Miss Johnson: "Yes, I could, but I promised I wouldn't."

• The news reporter asked the 105-year-old man for advice on how to reach such a ripe old age.

The old man answered, "Nothing to it. Just drink at least one shot of whiskey every day."

"But lots of people drink whiskey every day," the reporter said, "and yet they die long before they reach old age. How do you explain that?"

"Simple," the old man shrugged. "They don't keep doin' it long enough."

• First Farmer: "I quit plowing for dinner every day at exactly eleven-thirty."

Second Farmer: "Do you have a wristwatch or a pocket watch?"

First Farmer: "Don't have neither one. The whistle at the sawmill blows ever' day at noon; so I just quit thirty minutes before I hear it."

• Passenger to airline ticket agent: "I want my brown suitcase sent to Los Angeles, my green suitcase sent to Kansas City, my tan suitcase sent to Albuquerque, and my golf clubs sent to Fairbanks."

Ticket agent: "I'm sorry, sir; this flight is to San Francisco. We can't do that."

Passenger: "Why not? You did it last time."

• Lawyer: "I wonder what our ancestors would think of our country today?"

Dentist: "When I get to heaven, I'll ask them."

Lawyer: "But what if they didn't go to heaven?"

Dentist: "Well, in that case, you ask them."

Famous Last Words:

• "Let's see if it's loaded."

• "Gimme a match. I think the pilot light is out."

• "We can make it easy. I don't even see a train."

• "If you knew anything at all, you wouldn't be a traffic cop."

• "What's this red button for?"

• Don't worry. My husband won't be home until tomorrow."

DUBLIN'S GREAT STORYTELLERS

We have great storytellers in this area, like Joe Durant, Bucky Tarpley, Judy Thomas, Paul Kellam, Georgia Snipes, M. C. Tapley, "Stormin' Norman" Bond, G. C. Hawkins, Ross Sheppard, Jack Thomas, and "Mo" Darsey, to name a few.

Some say they can't remember jokes. Try this: Don't try to remember the joke. Just memorize the punch line. You can always improvise if you know the punch line.

How many times have you heard the same joke told by several people within a few weeks? The body of the joke will vary, but the punch line will invariably remain the same.

At times something intended to be serious comes out as humor due to an error in delivery by a nervous speaker. Here are two examples:

• The presiding officer was introducing the governor of the Virgin Islands at a government seminar when he said: "Ladies and Gentlemen, I am extremely pleased and honored to have the privilege of presenting our distinguished speaker—the virgin of Governor's Island."

• Closer to home, this came from the lips of Dublin radio personality Bucky Tarpley more than thirty years ago when he was a radio neophyte in Dublin.

Each day Bucky would give this introduction to the Noon News a few seconds before twelve o'clock: "And now it's time for a look at the Noon News and the market nationwide."

It came out this way: "And now, it's time for a look at the Nude News and the naked Martians!"

This story comes from Mo Darsey:

• Two vagrants, R. J. and Roy Lee, who were obviously pretty much in the same sauce, stopped at a farmhouse near Sarasota, Florida, and knocked on the back door. A lady appeared.

"We was wonderin', ma'am, if you got any work we could do to make a little money f'r somethin' t' eat," R. J. said.

"We been outta' work for a while, and we're hungry," said Roy Lee.

"Well," said the lady, "there's a pile of stovewood over by the chicken house. If you want to split it, I'll cook you some lunch."

It was agreed. R. J. and Roy Lee shuffled off toward the wood-pile.

The lady began to cook and watched R. J. and Roy Lee dutifully, although reluctantly, taking turns splitting the wood. Then the telephone rang.

The caller was a lady scheduled to speak to a women's study group at the woman's home that afternoon at 3:00 P.M. She called to report that she had laryngitis and would be unable to speak.

"Oh, my goodness!" exclaimed the hostess. "What will I do about a program?"

After appropriate apologies the caller hung up, leaving the farm wife in a dither. But then, fate intervened.

She looked out the kitchen window and saw Roy Lee drop the axe, do two back flips, grab his left foot with his right hand, hop on one leg some twenty feet toward the chicken house, jump an eight-foot fence, run into a tractor, roll over twice, shimmy to the roof of the chicken house, let out a blood-curdling Tarzan yell, and plunge headlong into a haystack—never releasing his grip on his foot with his right hand.

"Amazing!" thought the farm wife, subconsciously thinking "circus," "acrobat," and "the women's club meeting."

She yelled to R. J., who was standing nonchalantly atop the woodpile leaning on the axe while watching Roy Lee go through his paces. "Do you think your friend would do that again for a hundred dollars?"

"Don't know," R. J. said, "but I'll ask him."

"Please do!" she pleaded.

"Hey! Roy Lee!" R. J. yelled.

"What is it?" Roy Lee moaned.

"You wanna' cut off another toe for a hundred dollars?"

GOOD JOKES DON'T HAVE TO BE DIRTY

How many joke books are there in America's bookstores? Probably thousands, and many of the jokes are repeats.

I collect joke books so it was a pleasant surprise for me to return home one night and find two books behind my door that had been left there by a nice lady. One was a collection of jokes by Homer Rodeheaver titled *F'r Instance*. It was published in 1947.

It is both refreshing and enjoyable. Refreshing because of its clean, family-type jokes and enjoyable because of the simple manner in which they are presented.

Some may think many of the jokes and stories old-fashioned or strait-laced. Not me. I have long held that the best jokes and stories are clean jokes and stories. And the jokes have obviously weathered the storm for the past forty-five years because many of the ones in *F'r Instance* appear in several of my joke books, some less than two years old. If you're looking for something sexy or dominated by four-letter words, you should read no further. I keep the book on my coffee table and won't hide it when my son, daughter, and grandsons come to visit.

Now for a look at a few jokes from the midforties:

• *Boy came to fish:* The small boy had fallen into the stream but had been rescued. "How did you come to fall in?" asked a bystander. "I didn't come to fall in," the boy explained. "I came to fish and fell off that log."

• *Dividing the apples:* "If your mother gave you a large apple and a small apple and told you to divide with your brother, which one would you give him?" asked the teacher.

"Do you mean my big brother or my little one?" asked the boy.

• *Long-winded master of ceremonies:* After the emcee had rambled on and on, far into the night, he finally said, "And now Mark Twain will favor us with his address."

The humorist arose, smiled at the wearied audience, noted the lateness of the hour, bowed politely, and said: "128 Tremont Street, Boston, Massachusets." Then he sat down.

• *Druggist's mistake:* "You made a mistake in that prescription for my mother-in-law," said the customer. "Instead of quinine, you used strychnine."

"You don't say!" said the druggist. "In that case you owe me twenty cents more!"

• *Long-staying guest:* The guest was getting ready to depart. The hour was well past midnight. "Goodnight," he said. "I hope I haven't kept you up too late."

Host (yawning): "Not at all. We would have been getting up soon anyway."

• *The honest co-ed:* Every year college deans pop the routine question to their undergraduates: "Why did you come to college?"

Usually the answers are as trite as the question; but one young co-ed from a small rural community answered thusly when the question was put to her. "Well, I came to be went with, but I ain't yet."

• *Not well:* The doctor confided to the patient's wife, "Your husband won't ever be able to work again."

"I'll go tell him," she said. "That will cheer him up."

I was having lunch one Sunday with a preacher friend and his wife. The subject of jokes came up, as it usually does when I'm with a preacher. He's a great joke teller. But this time it was his wife, Carol, who occupied center stage.

We were talking about eating out and about how the dining habits of Americans have changed over the past thirty years when Carol said:

"Right. I know a mother of three small children who works and every time she yells 'OK, kids! It's supper time!' the kids run and jump in the car."

And then the preacher husband, Bill, countered with this one: "Well, let me tell you this. Every time Carol cooks, the smoke alarm goes off!"

He'll probably live to regret having said that.

Here are a few more you might enjoy:

• A barber with a bad case of "morning after the night before" shakes nicked the customer he was shaving. The customer flinched and growled, "There! You see what too much liquor will do to you?"

"Yeah," replied the barber. "It sure makes your skin tender."

• An aged woman, born and nurtured in the South, was endeavoring to impress upon her nephews and nieces the beauties of the South and its people, when one of the nephews spoke up.

"Auntie," he asked, "do you think that all the virtues originated in the South and have been preserved by the southern people?"

"No, not all, but most of them," she replied.

"Do you think that Jesus Christ was a Southerner?" asked a young niece.

The old lady hesitated a moment then said, "Well, He was good enough to be a Southerner!"

• Colleges and insane asylums both are mental institutions in a way. But one has to show some improvement to graduate from an asylum.

• Friend: "Has your son's college education proved helpful since you took him into your firm?"

Father: "Oh, yes, whenever we have a board meeting, we let him mix the cocktails."

• Young boy on telephone to dentist's receptionist: "My mother told me to call and make an appointment with the dentist."

Receptionist: "Sorry, the dentist is out this week."

Young boy: "When will he be out again?"

• A state trooper stopped a speeding truck in South Georgia and asked the driver: "Say fella, don't you have a governor on that truck?"

"No, sir!" replied the truck driver. "That's fertilizer you smell!"

• Teacher: "How old would a person be who was born in 1920?"

Smart pupil: "Man or woman?"

• The judge, with many years' experience, pounded his gavel for the court to come to order, then turned to the woman in the witness box:

"The witness will please state her age," he ordered, "after which she will be sworn in."

• "Your name, please?" asked the census taker.

"Matilda Brown," answered the woman.

"And your age?" he pursued.

"Have the Hill sisters next door given you their ages?" she asked.

"No," said the census taker.

"Well, I'm the same age as they."

"That will do," said the census taker.

Then, as he proceeded to fill out the form, the woman saw him write, "Matilda Brown, as old as the Hills."

• An expert army marksman passed through a small town and saw evidence of amazing shooting. On trees, walls, fences, and barns were numerous bull's-eyes with bullet holes in the exact center. He stopped and asked if he might meet the remarkable marksman.

The man turned out to be the village idiot. "This is the most wonderful marksmanship I've ever seen," said the army man. "How in the world do you do it?"

"Easy as pie," the fella said. "I shoot first and draw the bull's-eye afterward."

• A professor who had taught for many years was counseling a young teacher.

"You will discover," he said, "that in nearly every class there will be a youngster eager to argue. Your first impulse will be to silence him, but I advise you to think carefully before doing so. He is probably the only one listening."

• The policeman stopped a man walking down a back street clad only in his undershorts.

"Where are you going?" asked the policeman.

"Home."

"Where have you been?"

"Playing poker at the club."

"Oh? So you're a poker player, are you?"

"No, I'm not," replied the man, "but I just left six fellows who are."

A FEW WORDS OF WISDOM FROM HENRY

My Atlanta pen pal Henry Bowden is an eighty-two-year-old attorney and sage who writes humorous tidbits for the sheer enjoyment of it. In his latest collection he advises that these should be memorized as they may come in handy one day:

• Early to bed and early to rise, and you'll never have red in the whites of your eyes.

• Lots of folks ask for criticism, but what they really want is praise.

• A Methodist preacher named Tweedle, refused an honorary degree, not that he didn't like Tweedle, but he couldn't stand Tweedle, D.D.

• Babies heads have no hair,
  Old men's heads are just as bare.
  So between the cradle and the grave,
  Life's just a haircut and a shave.

• No longer docked if he is late,
  No longer required to report at eight;
  Knowing that time no longer was required,
  They gave him a watch when he retired.

• He who hoots with the owls at night cannot soar with the eagles in the morn.

• Confidence is the feeling you sometimes have before you fully understand the situation.

• Show me a man with both feet on the ground, and I'll show you a man who can't get his pants on.

• You know money is a great deal like manure. If you spread it around, it does a lot of good; but if you just pile it up, it stinks.

• Oratory is the art of making deep noises from the chest that sound like important messages from the brain.

• A bell is not a bell until you ring it.
  A song is not a song until you sing it.
  Love in your heart is not put there to stay.
  Love is not love until you give it away.

• One of my doctor friends told me of the difficulty he had in getting started in his profession back in the 1930s. He said that times were so tough that he had to share a thermometer with another young doctor down the hall from him. One worked in the morning and the other in the afternoon. He also said that money was so scarce that his stethoscope was on a party line.

• Often you can tell by listening to a telephone receptionist whether she is a local girl or from way off somewhere. Those from way off somewhere will answer the telephone and say, "Will you please remain on the line, he will be with you shortly." The ones from around here will say, "Just hold on, he'll talk to you in a minute or two."

Also, the girl from way off will say, "May I tell him who's calling?" But the local girl will say, "What's your name? I'll tell him you're on the line."

• I used to go to a number of cocktail parties, but no more. You know what a cocktail party is, don't you? That's where sandwiches and people are cut into little pieces.

Also, invariably some lady will approach me and say, "I am so glad to see you, Henry. I'm Naomi, Jerome's wife."

Well and good, but who in the heck is Jerome?

• Show me a home where the Buffalo roam, and I'll show you a dirty house.

THE ART OF WRITING

There are writers and then there are writers. I guess it matters not how you write as long as you get your message across. Like the fourth-grade girl who lived in a very wealthy neighborhood and was asked by her teacher to write a story about a poor family. That night she sat in her room and pondered her assignment. Finally, she began to write: "This family was very poor. The mommy was poor. The daddy was poor. The brothers and sisters were poor. The upstairs maid was poor. The downstairs maid was poor. The nurse was poor. The cook was poor. The butler was poor. The yardman was poor. The gardener was poor. The chauffeur was poor . . ."

There you have it. I guess we all write about life as we see it.

Then, there was the sixth-grade youngster who replied to the test question, "What is a will and what purpose does it serve?" with this answer: "A will is a written document in which a dead person tells how he wants his property divided among his errors."

Youngsters have no monopoly on making errors while writing or speaking. So much for the kids. Let's take a look at the grownups:

• Take the husband and wife who decided it was time to start spelling out words to each other that they didn't want their three-year-old daughter to hear.

"Hello, dear! What kind of day did you have?" asked the wife.

"Boy!" said the husband as he wiped his brow, "I had one hell of a D-A-Y!"

How do we write? Take a look at the following sentences, reportedly taken from actual correspondence received by one of the social service agencies in a large American metropolis:

• "I have no children as my husband is a truck driver and works day and night."

• "In accordance with your instructions, I have given birth to twins in the enclosed envelope."

143

- "My husband is unable to work and I have Affa Davis to prove it."

- "Why do you say I appear to be Oblivious when my forms clearly say I'm a Baptist?"

- "Please send my money at once because I have left town and have no forwarding address."

- "Enclosed find my files which I have lost. Can you find them for me?"

- "My sister and her seven children live with me and I can prove it if you will just come by my house and listen."

- "I am forwarding my marriage certificate and six children, all of whom were baptized, on half a sheet of paper."

- "I am writing to say that my baby was born two years old. When do I get my money?"

- "Mrs. Wilson has not had any clothes for almost a year and as a result is being visited regularly by members of the clergy."

- "I am happy to report to you that my husband, who is missing, is dead."

- "This is my eighth child. What are you going to do about it?"

- "Please let me know for certain if my husband is alive. I am living with my boyfriend and he can't eat, sleep or do nothing until he knows."

- "I am very much annoyed that you have the nerve to brand my son illiterate. That is a dirty lie! I was married almost three weeks before he was born."

- "In answer to your letter, I have given birth to a ten-pound boy. I hope this meets your requirements."

- "I am forwarding my marriage certificate and three children, one of which you can see was a mistake."

- "You changed my little boy to a little girl. Will this make any difference?"

- "Unless I get my husband's money pretty soon, I will be forced to live an immortal life."

TIME TO PUT OLD GRAY MATTER TO WORK

Try these mind-bogglers. There are no tricks or deceit involved. All have logical solutions. Trust me. Solutions are at the end:

(1) As I was going to St. Ives, I met a man with seven wives. Every wife had seven sacks, in the sacks were seven cats. Every cat had seven kittens. Every kitten had a mouse in tow.

How many were going to St. Ives?

(2) A man appeared at a prison on visiting day to visit a male prisoner, only to be told by the guard that only immediate relatives were permitted to visit. The visitor then said, "Brothers and sisters have I none, but that man's father is my father's son."

The guard then let him in. What was the relationship of the prisoner to the visitor?

(3) Is there biological justification for a man not marrying his widow's sister?

(4) Two men are playing Trivial Pursuit. They play three games and each wins the same number of times yet none of the games is a draw or a default.

How did that happen?

(5) What five-letter word is pronounced the same even after you delete four of its letters?

(6) What common household and office item often displays the fraction $24/31$?

(7) The person who made it had no use for it; the person who bought it didn't want it; and the one who finally ended up with it never knew about it.

What was it?

(8) What is the only letter in the alphabet you wouldn't need to spell the names of all fifty states?

(9) In top to bottom traffic lights, which color is on the bottom?

(10) Are there more red or white stripes in the American flag?

(11) What letters of the alphabet have been omitted

from the telephone dial?

(12) Think of your closest friend. He or she can sit somewhere that you'll never be able to sit.

Where is it?

(13) Every autumn day John raked the back yard leaves into fifteen piles and the front yard leaves into eleven piles. Then, he'd rake them all together in the side yard.

How many piles would there be in John's side yard?

(14) Pitney High defeated Bowles High in a basketball game, 110–34.

Pete, Harry, John, Phil, and Stan scored the most points in Pitney's history.

The five starters went 8, 10, 22, 28, and 30. From the following clues, can you figure out who scored how many points?

The 30 points weren't made by Pete. Everyone scored more points than Pete.

The 28 points weren't made by Harry, who scored two points more than Phil.

Stan scored fewer points than John.

(15) How many successful jumps must a paratrooper make before he graduates from jump school?

Answers: (1) One; (2) The prisoner is the visitor's son; (3) Yes. As his widow's husband, he's dead; (4) They weren't playing each other; (5) Queue; (6) A calendar; (7) A coffin; (8) Q; (9) Green; (10) Red—There are seven reds and six whites; (11) Q and Z; (12) In your lap; (13) One; (14) Harry scored the most points—30; Phil scored two fewer than Harry—28; John scored 22; Stan scored 10; Pete scored 8; (15) All of them.

PART SIX

POLITICS: THE BIGGEST JOKE OF ALL

I've read this section time and time again. With each reading one question surfaces: Can the United States of America afford Washington, D.C.?

The answer is always the same: a resounding No!

I don't understand politics or politicians. We cuss 'em but keep electing the same ones that did it to us over and over again. And you can't insult a politician. He'll simply smile at your insult and keep on shakin' hands, palms up.

I particularly like the story of the teacher who asked each student in her fourth-grade class on the first day of school the father's occupation. She heard doctor, preacher, factory worker, store owner, stock broker, and others.

Finally, she came to one little boy and asked the question, "And what is your father's occupation, William?"

"My daddy plays the piano in a whorehouse," was his reply.

The teacher was horrified, and that very night she went to the fashionable home of the little boy, rang the doorbell, and introduced herself to the man who answered the door, identifying himself as little William's father.

"Won't you come in?" the father asked.

"No, thank you," the teacher said tersely. "I can ask you what I'd like to ask here."

"And what is that?"

"Can you tell me why your son William would characterize your

147

profession as that of being a piano player in a whorehouse?" she demanded to know.

"Well, you wouldn't want me to tell my ten-year-old son that his father is a lawyer and politician, would you?"

The common man has been fighting the politicians, and losing, for years. It is an accepted way of life. We send 'em to the trough and feed 'em. Once they get used to living off the government sugar teat, there ain't no weaning 'em.

One young girl was overheard saying to another in a posh Washington restaurant, "What I'm looking for is a man who will treat me as if I were a voter and he was a candidate."

I could never run for president of the United States, and some of those who have been elected shouldn't have. I'll tell you here why I could never run. I'll tell you why I don't want to be president. I want to be king. I'll tell you why an errant petticoat convinced me to vote for George Bush rather than Bill Clinton. I'll let you in on a proposed new cabinet. I'll show you how we can indeed cut the deficit, but won't. Too sensible. I'll tell you why I think we need some representatives of the working class in Congress. And . . . a lot more about the political scene.

LET'S PUT THE WORKING CLASS IN CONGRESS

Right here at the outset let me say that I am not an economic adviser, a political consultant, a political analyst, or an expert on anything related to politics or government. What I am is an observer of government and politics, and I have come to the conclusion that government has become a four-letter word, and I'm not talking about "gov't." It's a much stronger word than that.

Take the U.S. Congress, for example. A recent CNN poll reported that 73 percent of those polled were dissatisfied with it. Only 73 percent? That's amazing. Who made up the other 27 percent, relatives and staffers?

The more I observe the action, or inaction, of Congress, the more I'm convinced that there are problems with this august group. One problem, as I see it, is that there are no working-class men and women in their ranks. Another problem is the division between the Republicans and the Democrats. Just let the Republicans make a proposal, and the Democrats shoot holes in it. Let the Democrats make a proposal and the Republicans blow it out of the water. The only thing they have agreed on recently is a hefty pay raise, about 35 percent.

For years the Congress dealt in millions. That's no more than pocket change in congressional jargon today. Millions jumped to billions, and then to trillions. To those of us who know not of such vast numbers it is no more than added zeroes. And there is little doubt in my mind that government is run by special interest groups and bureaucrats.

The special interest groups who are plundering more and more from the public treasury have elected their representatives to office because you and I have taken an apathetic attitude and let them get away with it. This happens when only 51 percent of the registered voters bother to go to the polling places. The bureaucrats, about 18 million strong, have taken over the apparatus of government; and their main efforts seem to be devoted to finding new ways to spend more money. And they will resist, even sabotage, any effort to reduce their little empires.

Now then, back to the Congress. There is little doubt that it is in trouble with the people. The Congress today enjoys the respect and believability of a flim-flam artist or a carnival barker. Like government, Congress has fallen into disrepute and distrust. There are those who say it is a disgrace. I won't go that far—not yet.

Congress is made up of career politicians, all very wealthy. They live off the fat of the land and may well be the most pampered 535 individuals in America. But we keep sending them back. That's the mystery to me. One thing catches their eye instantly, a red light on a television camera. They fly to it like homing pigeons and milk it for all it's worth. Just turn your television set on and see for yourself. Many of them live with C-Span and CNN. And have you ever noticed what happens on C-Span when the camera is focused on what is known in the House of Representatives as "Special Orders"? This comes when the business of the day is finished and any member can address the legislature for up to one hour. The only problem is that there is nobody listening. All the seats are empty, but the speakers ramble on and on.

Finally, why are there no working-class people in Congress? Simple. They don't have the money to run, and PAC money is not earmarked for the working class. We desperately need some poor and middle-class people in Congress. How can the likes of Ted Kennedy and Jay Rockefeller relate to the poor and middle class? They can't. The crisis comes to the poor and middle class when there is not enough food on the table, but it comes to the Congress when the Chivas Regal and vintage wines are dangerously low.

UPDATE ON THE LITTLE RED HEN

Several years ago I used something in my column that appeared in a hardware trade paper. It was "The Story of the Little Red Hen," with a slant. It was submitted to the paper initially by Charles W. Wedeking, owner of Wedeking True-Value Hardware in Dale, Indiana, a small town of 1,113.

It seems to me that with times the way they are today it might be well to include it here. While I make no pretense of understanding government, the economy, inflation, and the like, "The Little Red Hen" at least gives me some insight into where we were—and where we've come. Nothing has really changed, it has just become more confusing.

Many of you will no doubt remember the story from your childhood days. This version is a little different, definitely in keeping with the times, and it sounds all too familiar.

The Story of the Little Red Hen

Once upon a time, a little red hen scratched around and found some grains of wheat. She then proceeded to call her neighbors and said: "If we plant this wheat we'll have bread to eat. Who will help me plant it?"

"Not I," mooed the cow.

"Not I," quacked the duck.

"Not I," grunted the pig.

"Not I," honked the goose.

So the little red hen planted the wheat herself. It grew and ripened well, and she asked, "Who will help me reap my wheat?"

"Not I," said the duck. "I'm on annual leave."

"Not I," said the pig. "That's not in my classification."

"Not I," said the cow. "I'd lose my seniority."

"Not I," said the goose. "I'd lose my unemployment compensation."

So the little red hen continued to toil, reaping the wheat all alone. And when it came time to bake the bread, she asked, "Who will help me bake my bread?"

"It would be overtime for me," said the cow.

"I'm a dropout and don't know how," squealed the pig.

"I'd lose my food stamp benefits," quacked the duck.

"It would be discrimination if I were nothing more than a helper," honked the goose."

Undaunted, the little red hen baked the bread herself. It turned out beautifully and everyone wanted some. In fact, each demanded a share. But the little red hen refused, saying she would eat the bread herself.

"Excess profits!" bellowed the cow.

"Capitalist leech!" cried the duck.

"I demand equal rights!" yelled the goose.

The pig just snorted and grunted; and they all marched around the little red hen, throwing mean looks her way and calling her dirty names.

"We demand arbitration!" they chanted repeatedly in unison. The scene was becoming nasty.

A neighbor made a quick call to Washington and a government agent arrived on the scene by helicopter just in the nick of time.

"You must not be greedy," he admonished the little red hen, as he reached in his briefcase for a pad and pencil.

"But I earned this bread," said the little red hen, meekly.

"Right. I agree," said the government agent. "Anyone in America can earn and accumulate as much as he wants. But under our new government regulations, workers must divide their excess products with the unfortunate. It's the American way," he explained as he glanced at the cow, the duck, the pig and the goose, who were all smiling.

Actually they all lived together happily ever after; but to this day no one in government can understand why the little red hen never bakes bread anymore.

The little story makes me wonder if anyone in government will ever figure it out.

A FEW IDEAS FOR CUTTING THE DEFICIT

I received a letter from ten-year-old Brandon Register, who is interested in a writing career. Brandon wrote that President Clinton has an 800 number to accommodate citizens desiring to call him with complaints, suggestions, or commentary in general. Just leave a recorded message.

"I doubt that President Clinton sits around all day listening to the more than sixty thousand calls a day that come in," Brandon wrote.

I don't have the 800 number, but if I did I would call with a few suggestions regarding the president's proposed spending cuts and tax increases to reduce the deficit. Mr. Clinton obviously needs all the help he can get in this area.

Here are a few suggestions, Mr. President:

• Close the White House kitchen. You made a big deal during your campaign of stopping at McDonald's for Big Macs. Of course, the media were always present for what is known in political jargon as a photo op to show you breaking bread with the common man. Now you're stuck with it. In the eyes of a common man, you're a Big Mac man.

The White House kitchen is obsolete. Rock Cornish Hens in Grenadine, Quiche Lorraine, Broiled Tomatoes Oregano, Fettucini Alfredo, Blueberries in Sour Cream, and all the other exotic recipes left over from the two previous Republican administrations will have to go.

Just jog on down to the nearest McDonald's and pig out, or send a Secret Service agent for a dozen or so Big Macs.

Of course, the state dinner menus will have to be considered. I've done that. simply upgrade to Krystals and figure on, oh, about six per guest along with a small order of fries. Include a few chili pups for Hillary, who will want to be different.

• Terminate the White

House groundskeeper. Let First Brother Roger cut the grass. Equip him up with a Walkman and a Snapper Comet, point him in the right direction, and let him listen and cut to his heart's content.

• Eliminate the White House limousine fleet. Sell the limos to the Mafia, the Academy Awards committee, or a few country music types like Billy Ray Cyprus, or whatever his name is. You know, the guy that gave us the worst song, "Achy Breaky Heart," since John Anderson's "Swinging" a few years back.

• Cut the salaries of congressmen 75 percent. They don't need the money. If they weren't wealthy, they wouldn't be in Congress in the first place. Besides, they can live off the lobbyists like Georgia legislators do.

Have you ever seen a W-2 congressman, Mr. President? No, and you never will. Only the rich need apply.

• Enact legislation to allow the people to vote on the salaries of congressmen, ambassadors, cabinet members, and government consultants.

• Immediately reduce your salary from $200,000 to $35,000. You boasted long and loud during the campaign that as governor of Arkansas your salary was $35,000 per year. Can't you make do with that now since everything you need is gratis?

• Impose a sin tax of one dollar on all mixed drinks purchased in bars "inside the beltway" by congressmen, bureaucrats, and their staff members. That alone should cut the deficit in half.

• Assess a fee of five dollars for every "my colleague," "distinguished gentlemen," or "the other side of the aisle" uttered by congressmen when on C-Span.

• Order the Federal Communications Commission to monitor all radio and television interviews of athletes and impose a fine of five dollars for each "you know" spoken on the air.

• Add a five-dollar nuisance tax to every ticket sold to a rock, rap, or Madonna concert.

Just call me if you need me, Mr. President. I'm full of ideas and other things.

WHY I WILL NEVER RUN FOR PRESIDENT

After watching President George Bush and Arkansas Governor Bill Clinton during the 1992 presidential campaign, I've decided it must be tough for a presidential candidate out there on the campaign trail knowing that a horde of news reporters are camped in his hometown for the duration, searching for anything suspicious or degrading. Gary Hart is a good example. He was driven from the race as a candidate for the Democratic nomination, largely by his own doing, when reporters dug up his association with Donna Rice. A boat trip to the island of Bimini and photographs of him and Ms. Rice, she sitting on his lap, did him in. But I said then and I still say that Hart was the best candidate in that race in 1988. And what is he doing now? I don't know.

Before the 1992 election, the media managed to dig up three pieces of information regarding Bill Clinton that required an explanation.

First, there was his alleged twelve-year romantic affair with Gennifer Flowers. She reportedly received $175,000 for selling her story to *Star*, a supermarket tabloid. She also produced taped telephone conversations, supposedly with Clinton, but the jury is still out regarding the authenticity of the story and tapes.

Next, the gravediggers came up with the fact that Clinton allegedly made every effort to avoid serving in the military during the Vietnam war. Clinton explains this by admitting that he applied for and received a deferment, but later asked to be made available for the draft and produced a letter to that effect.

Finally, his opponent alleged during a nationally televised debate of the Democratic candidates that as governor Clinton had steered government legal business to his wife's law firm. This was hotly denied by Clinton.

It seems that in this day and time what a candidate stands for is not as important as what he has done in the past that can be dug up and publicized.

I don't think I would want to run for president, and I don't understand why others do it. I can see it now if I should choose to run and the gravediggers started digging. The tabloids would be filled with my indiscretions, like these:

- Whaley reportedly put a cow in the commandant's office at Georgia Military College in 1944.
- Information uncovered that Whaley doesn't wear pajamas.
- Teacher says Whaley stuck chewing gum under desk.
- Whaley spotted spitting on sidewalk in 1939.
- According to witnesses, Whaley pops chewing gum in public.
- Whaley seen working in flower bed during golf tournament.
- Eyewitness says Whaley seen striking match before closing cover.
- Whaley observed in library dog-earing book pages.

I WANT TO BE KING, NOT PRESIDENT

I've never wanted to be president. Actually, I want to be king. And when I take over there will be some changes:

- All junk mail can be marked "Return to Sender," and the company that sent it will have to pay the Postal Service for bringing it back.
- No professional athlete will be paid more than a schoolteacher. Same thing with movie stars.
- School teaching, not administrating, will be the highest paid profession in the country.
- If you get a traffic ticket for anything (speeding, stop sign, anything) you lose your driver's license for a month, plus whatever fines the judge deems appropriate.
- Another traffic ticket, and you lose your license for another month.

Of course this will obviously spark a need for public transportation, which means fewer accidents, cleaner air, and less highway repair. (Possums will also live longer, though I haven't figured out yet if this is a good thing.)

- Drunk driving? First offense—you lose your license forever. Second offense—you go to prison forever. Third offense—won't be none, will there?
- TV commercials will have small disclaimers admitting that this "typical" family is actually a group of unrelated actors and their real homes (in fact, nobody's home) don't look this nice.

This may be a little extreme, because I think TV commercials show more originality and better acting than most TV programs. These will continue to be aired, but only to prison inmates.

- The Braves will always be in the World Series. If they can't win the pennant outright, then we'll move the World Series here, anyway, and the National League city

157

that loses will get the Super Bowl which, while lucrative, is always over-hyped and dull.

• The Minnesota Twins will either move back to their old, outdoor stadium or return the franchise to Washington, which they abandoned in 1961.

• As king, I will not only throw out the ceremonial "first pitch" of the season, I'll get to play right field and bat cleanup. (Congressmen, considering their inherent value, will serve as parking lot attendants. Senators will be peanut vendors.)

• When I am king, TV weather-persons will have to admit they're just guessing.

• The work week won't begin until after lunch on Monday. It doesn't anyway.

• Telephone rings will be nothing more than a melodious little tinkle, sort of like the sound an elevator door makes upon reaching its floor. And they will be spaced ten seconds apart.

I've got a few more ideas, and I realize that there are those who figure I'm a little weak on foreign affairs. If so, you can take that subject up with my secretary of state, Clint Eastwood.

It will make his day.

LIFE ON THE CAMPAIGN TRAIL

Keeping up with the various candidates and their campaigns for president requires a lot of effort. Each election I see them either getting off an airplane at some airport or making the rounds and shaking hands with people in a diner. And it seems like one or two of them are on C-Span every day. It attracts them like flies.

There's something about a diner that draws candidates, even though I doubt that any of the candidates has eaten in a diner since first being elected to public office. They don't eat, of course. They just interrupt the common people, who are trying to eat and get back to work on time, and the waitresses who are serving the food. And have you ever noticed that presidential candidates never travel alone? Never. They always have a bunch of aides tagging along to do whatever a presidential candidate's aide does and to block the aisles, and the waitresses have a hard time getting to the booth or table with the food.

We don't have diners in South Georgia. We have cafés and restaurants, and I like them better than diners. But diners are big in the East, and there just flat ain't much walking space. I think it would be very frustrating to go in a diner in New Hampshire with an hour for lunch, and after being seated and ordering look up only to see a presidential candidate, his aides, several television crews, radio and newspaper people, and photographers walk in and start making the rounds, chatting about something the candidate has no interest in or knowledge of. He's just trying hard to convince those present that he's a good old boy and understands whatever area of the country he happens to be in. He shakes hands with everyone in the diner, including a few aides, and solicits their votes.

Meanwhile, the fella with the one-hour lunch break is getting a little restless. I mean, after all, he didn't go in the diner to shake hands and listen to politics. He went there to eat and only has fifteen minutes left, but still no lunch. The problem is that the cook filled the order and the waitress picked it up, but she can't find a way to get to his table. She tried going out the front door and coming in the back. No luck. Two television cameras are blocking the door. She tried walking on the counter with the guy's lunch in hand. No luck. Photographers are standing on it to get a better shot of the candidate.

The hungry diner now has but six minutes left on his lunch hour. He uses sign language and asks the waitress to put his lunch in a "to go" bag. She did just that and threw the bag to him. He threw a few dollar bills to her and turned to leave. As he reached the front door the candidate yells to him, "Nice to see you! Remember me in the primary!"

"Right! You can count on that!" the guy yells back over his shoulder.

In addition to diners, candidates show up at factories, schools, churches, shopping malls, and anywhere else where they might see ten or more people. But diners seem to be a favorite of all candidates.

Seldom will you see a candidate eating. I know they must eat, but I can't recall seeing one eat a full meal on television. I did see Pat Buchanan drinking a Coke once in a diner in New Hampshire and Bill Clinton eating a piece of cheesecake in Chicago—but neither paid. Who pays for the Cokes and cheesecake candidates eat?

And that brings up a few questions I'd like to have answered. Some of the candidates obviously hadn't been home in months. Who takes care of their laundry? Who pays the light bill? The water bill? Who cuts the grass? Who took care of the governing while the governor was gone? I'm sure each candidate has his own favorite barber back home, so who cuts his hair?

I don't know. It seems to me that we've reached the point where the only reason to label candidates Republican or Democrat is so we'll know who to vote against—not for.

WHY MY VOTE WENT TO BUSH

During the first week in October 1992, I wrote in my newspaper column that I would reveal my choice for president before the November 3rd election. After considering all the facts, promises, rhetoric, slander, dirty tricks, and so forth, I announced that I would vote for George Bush, although I was convinced that Bill Clinton would win. And I gave the reasons for my choice:

Times have changed. Television is now a major factor in influencing voter choices. No, that's not quite correct. Television is *the* major factor in influencing voter choices.

How many Bush/Quayle or Clinton/Gore bumper stickers did you see? I can't recall having seen a single one, but I didn't tune in to C-Span or CNN for a year without seeing either a candidate or a group of expert political analysts talking a mile a minute about the election.

Any candidate who fails to come across well on the tube has a strike against him from the beginning. Forget his qualifications. Forget who is the best man for the job. That has little, if anything, to do with the way voters make their choices.

I travel a great deal, and I listen to what people said about the candidates. Here are a few examples of the reasoning behind some voter choices:

● *Robbie Nell Bell,* from Alma (Robbie Nail Bail, from Almer: Formerly the head waitress and guardian of the jukebox at Mel's Juke, about a six-pack north of Broxton on U.S. 441. Also "Miss Georgia Redneck Queen" in 1987.)

Robbie Nell is now happily married, again, lives on a farm near Cadwell, Georgia, and works the second shift in a convenience store. Also, an avid television watcher:

"Well, I kin tail ya' this: I ain't votin' f'r no ticket with Al Gore on it. I don' lak his slicked down hair. I think he uses

Brilliantine on it. I used t' keep cump'ny with a ole boy fum Waycross whut used Brilliantine on his hair an' he dang near ruint the back o' my mamma's settee," Robbie Nell said. "Ya' kin scratch th' Clinton/Gore ticket. An' Mama ain't votin' f'r it neither. My mama's got a rail good mem'ry, mister."

● *Abner Boone*, Route 3, Wolfton, South Carolina. (Wolfton is just outside Orangeburg on U.S. Highway 21, right between Don't Litter and Resume Speed. Can't miss it. Zip Code? Forget it. Abner says he don't mess with 'em.)

Abner, an unlicensed liquor dealer, says, "Ain't votin' this year. Back in '88 th' Dukakis crowd gimmee' a pint o' Ol' Crow, a five-dollar bill, two packs o' Red Man, an' a Elvis Presley poster th' night 'fore th' 'lection. I ain't heared nuthin' so far this time aroun'. Mus' be th' 'conmy. I'm waitin' til '96 when Jack Kemp runs agin' Sam Nunn."

● *Ruthie Mae Gilbert*, General Delivery, Soddy-Daisy, Tennessee. (Soddy-Daisy is just north of Chattanooga on U.S. 27 between Falling Water and Sale Creek. It is one of the few towns that can't be seen from Lookout Mountain.)

Ruthie Mae is retired. She's now a television addict. She formerly owned and operated the Silk and Honey Massage Parlor on 8th Avenue in Nashville, but was forced to close up shop a few years ago after she rubbed a Nashville vice officer the wrong way.

"Oh, my goodness! I just don't know, honey. I know Al Gore too well; Clinton and Bush are both left-handed, and that was a handicap in my trade. Bush can't seem to keep nothin' on his stomach; Quayle don't like Murphy Brown, which is my fav'rite TV show," Ruthie Mae explained. "I may not go to the polls this year. I'll jus' hav' t' wait an' check th' *TV Guide* an' see whut's on th' tube November 3rd."

How and Why I Chose to Vote for Bush

I made my choice after much deliberation and in-depth study. I watched the candidates closely for months before deciding on Bush. But it wasn't Bush himself that turned the tide. It was his wife, Barbara. The candidates' wives were big in 1992.

I saw George and Barbara at the televised debate in Lansing, Michigan. It was after Bush had spoken and was leaving the speaker's platform with Barbara in tow that I made my decision to vote for him. And a logical decision it was, too.

Much was said of family values during the campaign, and as Barbara was walking to a waiting presidential limousine I couldn't help but notice that her slip was showing from beneath the light blue dress she always wears. Unlike Nancy Reagan, who had hundreds of designer dresses at her disposal, Barbara apparently only owns one—the light blue one.

When I noticed that Mrs. Bush's slip was showing, a light came on upstairs; and I knew then and there I would vote for her husband. Why? Elementary, my dear Watson. Because the wife of any candidate whose slip is showing on national television obviously has more important things on her mind than a wayward petticoat—things like raising a family and baking cookies.

On the other hand, Hillary, Tipper, and Marilyn also wear slips that show, but by design. Their designer dresses are slit to showcase a visible petticoat, one of the fads necessary in the fashion world of the 1990s.

I'm sure the thing that really cinched my vote for Bush was that when I saw Mrs. Bush's slip showing, I immediately thought about my grandmother, Mrs. Jessie (Wes) Whaley, who lived in an unpainted but often whitewashed house on sixteen acres of the poorest land in Hancock County, Georgia.

Grandma and Grandpa were in the dairy and livestock business, their herds consisting of two milk cows and a few goats whose number varied from month to month. Grandma milked the cows, churned, made butter, and sold it. She also baked and sold homemade cookies. Grandpa chewed tobacco, whittled, read *True Detective* magazines, and waited for the goats to reach marketable size.

When my grandmother sat sideways on her little stool and milked those two cows, her slip showed. When she churned, sang hymns, and made butter, her slip showed. When she stayed home and baked homemade cookies on her wood stove, her slip showed. When she sat in her rocker by the fireplace and sewed, her slip showed. She may well have owned the most visible slips in Hancock County.

Miss Jessie died when I was seventeen. I loved her dearly, and vice versa, but I don't recall ever having seen her when her slip wasn't showing. I also never once saw her lose her temper or frown. An angelic smile and an errant slip were her trademarks.

Every Sunday morning she and her husband were in their regular pew at Powelton Methodist Church. In most cases as they ascended the front steps leading to the church door this exchange took place between them:

"Jessie, your slip's showing."

"Spit out your tobacco before we go inside, Wes." And she tugged and he spat.

My grandmother concerned herself with the education of her seven children and their spiritual upbringing. All seven finished college, and at their graduations—although I wasn't yet born—I'd bet the egg money that Grandma's slip was showing, as well as her pride.

The lady had her priorities in order and a wayward slip was near the bottom of her list.

In April 1945, Miss Jessie went to heaven. Her husband and children have since joined her there. I wouldn't be surprised to learn one day that when she arrived her slip was showing, and that Saint Peter merely smiled and said, "Welcome, Miss Jessie. We've been expecting you."

Mr. Wes spit out his tobacco juice for the last time a month later and joined her.

I hope the nine of them will read this, and who am I to say they won't?

Somehow, I trust a grandmother whose slip shows. Would I buy a used car from one? You bet . . . as is.

Based on the above, I decided I would prefer to have Barbara Bush in the White House for four more years, so I voted for her husband. I think a visible slip worn by the First Lady is a good thing for the staid and tradition-rich mansion at 1600 Pennsylvania Avenue.

THE SCOOP FROM SHALLOW THROAT

It's a fact: No newspaper columnist can write effectively without sources. Sources are as important to a columnist as are perks to a congressman. Columnists just don't have as many.

I have sources—local, state, and national. We all do. Law enforcement officers call them informants. Columnists call them sources. In grade school we called them tattletales.

My prime source on the national scene is an excellent one, "of known reliability." He first told me about Donna Rice, Joe Biden, Gennifer Flowers, Charles Keating, and others. Each piece of information proved to be reliable.

His name is Shallow Throat. You do remember him, don't you? He's the guy of Watergate fame who sent Richard Nixon to the showers and completely cleaned out the White House with information furnished to investigative reporter Bob Woodard of the *Washington Post*.

Deep Throat has never been identified publicly, but I have my suspicions. He was about as close to the presidency as a guy could get, short of actually taking charge.

"Uncle Deep was my idol," Shallow said once. "He could dig up more dirt than a steam shovel."

Shallow is in a very sensitive position in Washington as a keeper of a government gladiolus garden, the location of which must understandably remain top secret. He also moonlights as a window dresser for a fashionable men's shop in Georgetown. But of prime importance is that his roommate, Sore Throat, is one of twelve trusted White House custodians whose job it is to take out the tons of trash that accumulate every day.

I hadn't heard from Shallow for several months, since the Gennifer fiasco. His call came shortly after midnight.

"Hello, Scoop?" (Shallow always calls me Scoop.)

"Yeah?"

"This is Shallow. How're ya' doin' down there?"

"Fine, just fine," I said. "Where are you?"

"I'm in a bar here in D.C., the Purple Pickle," he said. "Sore moonlights here, waiting on tables. Listen, Scoop, I've got a biggie for you."

"Yeah? What's that?"

"Strictly whisper stuff," he said softly. "Uncle Deep says it's dynamite. Sore came up with it early this morning."

"Well, want me to come up there and—?"

"Not necessary," Shallow interrupted. "Me and Sore are leaving in the morning for Florida to attend the Flowerama Festival at Primrose Beach. Sore will be the grand marshal of the parade on Saturday, and I'll be a pot plant judge. I looked at the map. We'll be coming right by Dublin on I-16, so how about meeting me next Monday night?"

"Sure, where? And how will I recognize you? I've only talked with you by telephone over the past several years so—"

"I've already thought about that. Here's the deal: I'll be wearing a lavender silk shirt with yellow polka dots, army fatigue trousers, and pink sneakers. And I'll have a silver earring in my left ear," Shallow said. "We'll be driving my pale green Volkswagen Beetle. According to the map, there's a rest stop on I-16 between Dudley and Dublin. I'll meet you at the rest stop at midnight and—"

"Uh . . . if it's all the same to you, Shallow, how about easing into a denim shirt, Levi jeans, Dingo boots, and a CAT Diesel cap. Stick a wad of Levi Garrett in your mouth and meet me in front of the Fuel City Truck Stop on I-75 at the Barnesville Exit, number 66."

"Well, if that's what you want Scoop."

"That's *exactly* what I want, Shallow."

"OK! OK! It's a done deal," Shallow conceded. "Monday night. Midnight. Fuel City Truck Stop. Denim shirt, Levi jeans, Dingo boots, CAT Diesel cap, and Levi Garrett. See you then. And Scoop, this is a biggie. It could make your career. Ta-ta."

SHALLOW THROAT SHOWS AND TELLS

I didn't expect Shallow Throat to show up at the Fuel City Truck Stop Monday night because of the storm. But at 11:55 P.M., his pale green Beetle skidded to a stop alongside pump number 8 (regular unleaded).

Shallow was in a denim shirt, Levi jeans, Dingo boots, and a black CAT Diesel cap. Thank goodness he had removed the earring.

He splattered tobacco juice like a pro, all over the trash can between pumps 6 (premium unleaded) and 7 (super unleaded). Some hit the diesel pump (number 1). Strong wind.

"I wasn't sure you'd make it," I said, "in view of the snow storm."

"Neither rain nor sleet," he said. "Sore couldn't make it. My first cousin, Strep, came with me. He's Uncle Deep's son, serving his apprenticeship."

"Hello, Strep. Ya'll wanna' eat?" I asked.

"No, thanks," Shallow said. "Here's the poop. It's dynamite, Scoop."

He handed me a manila envelope.

"What is it?"

"You'll see," Shallow said with a grin. "Sore picked it up at the Purple Pickle. The president left it in a back booth last week after she and her husband, Bill, stopped in with the Snake for a cold one."

"The Snake?"

"James Carville," he explained. "Everybody inside the Beltway calls him the Snake. It's a list of changes Carville and the president are making. She's not pleased with Bill's appointments. She says Bill promised change, and she's going to make some biggies. Read it, and then burn it. See ya' later, Scoop."

"Right. Thanks."

Here are the proposed changes:

Secretary of State .... William Buckley
Secretary of the Treasury .... Charles Keating
Secretary of Defense .... David Koresh
Attorney General .... Matlock
Secretary of the Interior .... Kim Basinger
Secretary of Agriculture .... James Kersey
Secretary of Commerce .... Ross Perot
Secretary of Labor Relations .... Frank Lorenzo
Co-Secretaries of Welfare .... Wyche Fowler
                                       Mack Mattingly
Secretary of Health .... Jack Kevorkian
Secretary of Education .... Eliot Wigginton
Secretary of Housing .... Leona Helmsley
Secretary of Transportation .... Ted Kennedy
Director, EPA .... Exxon Corporation
Drug Enforcement Agency Czar .... Marion Berry
Director, CIA .... Oliver North
Director, FBI .... Andy Griffith
Director, Secret Service .... Don Knotts
Director, INS .... Zoë Baird
Director, ATF .... Clint Eastwood
Director, Space Program .... Jonathan Winters
Director, Family Values Agency .... Woody Allen
Chief of Protocol .... Roseanne Barr Arnold
White House Chief of Staff .... Lee Iacocca
Speaker of the House .... James Stockdale
Director, FCC .... Howard Stern
Director, Banking and Finance .... Bert Lance
Director, Internal Revenue
    Service .... Donald Trump
Chairman, Civil Rights
    Commission .... Margie Schott
Director, OMB .... Any single mother of four
                                       with a monthly income of
                                       less than $500 a month
Chairman, Ethics Committee .... Bob Packwood
White House Communications
    Director .... Rush Limbaugh
Press Secretary .... Sam Donaldson
Alcohol and Beverage Control .... Lewis Grizzard
Surgeon General .... Dr. Ruth

PART SEVEN

THOSE WHO SERVE

I know of no professions that I hold in higher regard than those of preachers, farmers, and policemen. They serve their human beings.

My father was a Methodist preacher for forty-six years. He was also my best friend. He was a great storyteller and many of my best stories came from him. He died in November 1969. Do I miss him? Only twice a day—day and night.

I will always regret that he never wrote a book. He didn't have time. He was too busy ministering to his people.

Farmers are a special breed. Many of my best friends are men of the soil and share stories with me. Like this one:

A man owned a small farm in South Georgia. The Wage and Hour Department claimed he was not paying proper wages to his help and sent an agent to interview him.

The agent finally pointed his finger at the aging farmer and said curtly, "You just give me a list of your employees and tell me how much you pay them."

"All right," said the farmer. "I have a hired man. Been with me for three years. I pay him $600 a week, plus room and board. I have a cook. She's been here for six months. She gets $500 a week plus room and board."

"Anybody else?" asked the agent as he scribbled on a note pad.

"Yeah," the farmer said. "There's a half-wit here. Works about eighteen hours a day. I pay him ten dollars a week and give him chewing tobacco."

"Aha! I want to talk to that half-wit!" the agent roared.

"You're talkin' to him now," said the farmer.

And the policemen. Let it suffice to say that we should all say a prayer of thanks for them. They put their lives on the line for us every day and receive little in return other than the satisfaction of a job well done.

I have a soft spot in my heart for policemen. As an FBI agent for twenty years, I can never thank them enough for all the things they did for me—especially the one who saved my life.

'Nuff said.

DADDY'S NOTES

My father was a note saver. I'm glad he was. I wish he had put his collection, numbering in the hundreds, in the form of a book of some kind for others to read.

First, "The Preacher," that was surely written by one . . . or by his wife:

The Preacher

If he's young, he lacks experience; if he's old, he's "too old for our church."

If he has five or six children, he has too many; if he has none, he isn't setting a good example.

If his wife sings in the choir, she's being forward; if not, she's not interested in her husband's ministry.

If he uses a manuscript, he's preaching canned sermons and is dry; if he's extemporaneous, he rambles too much.

If he spends a lot of time in his study, he neglects his people; if he visits a lot, he's a gadabout.

If he's attentive to the poor, he's grandstanding; if to the wealthy, he's trying to be an aristocrat.

If he hunts or fishes, he's too worldly; if he doesn't, he's out of touch with the everyday world.

If he suggests improvements, he's a dictator; if he doesn't, he's merely a figurehead.

If he uses too many illustrations, he neglects the Bible; if not enough, he's not clear.

If he condemns wrong, he's cranky; if he doesn't, he's a compromiser.

If he preaches more than thirty minutes, he's long winded; if not, he's lazy.

If he fails to please everyone, he's hurting the church; if he does, he's hurting the church.

If he preaches tithing, he's money-hungry; if he doesn't, he's blamed for not meeting the church budget.

If he receives a large salary, he's mercenary; if a small one, it proves he's not worth much.

If he preaches every Sunday, people tire of hearing him; if he invites guest preachers, he's shirking his responsibility.

And there are those who think preachers have it easy. It takes much more than just showing up for a couple of hours Sunday morning.

Second, "Bag of Tools." I know this piece was very special to my dad. He used it often from his pulpit:

A Bag of Tools

Isn't it strange,
That princes and kings,
And clowns that caper in sawdust rings,
And common people,
Like you and me,
Are builders of eternity?
To each is given a bag of tools,
A shapeless mass,
And a book of rules,
And each must make,
Ere life has flown,
A stumbling block,
Or a stepping stone.

And finally, nobody enjoyed telling preacher stories more than my father. He was a mountain man. Storytelling was his forte, and I loved to listen to them when he told them. This was one of his favorites:

A young preacher serving his first church up in the North Georgia mountains was called upon to marry a young couple. It was his first wedding. He performed flawlessly, prompting the groom to compliment him in this manner:

"Preacher, ya' done real good. I'd like to give a few dollars, but I ain't got no money. So, I'll tell you what I'm gonna' do fer ya'. I got a old houn' dawg I been tryin' to sell for ten dollars. I'm gonna let you have him f'r five."

WHAT IS A FARMER?

Farmers are found in fields plowing up, seeding down, returning from, planting to, fertilizing with, spraying for, and harvesting it. Wives help them, little children follow them, city relatives visit them, salesmen detain them, meals wait for them, weather can delay them, but it takes heaven to stop them.

A farmer is a paradox. He's an overall executive with his home as his office; a scientist using fertilizer attachments; a purchasing agent in an old straw hat; a personnel director with grease under his fingernails; a production expert faced with a surplus; and a manager battling a price-cost squeeze.

A farmer likes sunshine, good food, state fairs, dinner at noon, Saturdays in town, family reunions, unbuttoned collars, and a good soaking rain in August. A farmer is not much for droughts, ditches, throughways, experts, weeds, the eight-hour day, helping with the housework, or insects.

Nobody else is so far removed from the telephone or so close to Mother Nature as is a farmer. Nobody else can remove everything from his pockets on washday and still overlook five staples, one cotter key, a rusty nail, three grains of corn, the stub end of a lead pencil, and chaff in each trouser cuff.

A farmer can fix things.

A farmer is a believer and a fatalist. He must have faith to meet the challenges of his capacities amid the possibility that an act of God like a late spring, an early frost, a tornado, a flood, or a drought can bring his business to a standstill. You can reduce his acreage, but you can't restrain his ambition.

And when he comes in from the field at noon for dinner, having spent the energy of his hopes and dreams, he can be recharged anew with three magic words: "The market's up."

- A farmer wears out two pairs of overalls growing enough cotton for one.
- Farmers are made of bent nails, rusty horseshoes, barbed wire, and held together with calluses.
- During planting time and harvest season, the farmer

finishes his forty-hour week by Tuesday noon; then, paining from a tractor-back, he somehow manages to put in another seventy-two.

● He buries last year's disappointments with springtime planting because he has faith not in himself alone. He'll finish a hard week's work, then drive five miles to church on Sunday.

● Some years it'll get too wet or too dry, or there'll be hail, wind, early frost, early snow, bugs, and bureaucrats. He may not even meet expenses. Yet the only lines in a farmer's face are from grinning through it all.

● The farmer remains the world's most stubborn optimist.

● The farmer plants in hope, cultivates in faith, and often ends in debt; then, he starts over with greater hope and stronger faith.

● Heaven help the family that depends on the farmer for support.

● Heaven help the nation that doesn't have him to support it.

I can't help but wonder at times why they keep at it with all the uncertainty that goes with farming, like government regulations and an unstable market for their goods.

● A farmer and his wife made one of their infrequent visits to the city and wandered into a very expensive and spiffy restaurant. The farmer inquired of the waiter as to the price of a hamburger.

"$5.75," said the waiter.

The farmer took out his pencil and began figuring on a napkin. Finished, he leaned over and whispered to his wife, "Martha, do you realize we've got a cow at home worth $85,000?"

● A farmer was plowing in a dry and dusty field in South Alabama one hot afternoon when a New Yorker pulled up in a big, shiny, chrome-plated car and said, "I can't see for the life of me how you make a living on this run-down farm."

The old farmer wiped his brow, spit out his chewing tobacco, and said, "Well, mister, let me tell you. I ain't as poor as you think. I don't even own this farm."

● "In my day," recalled the old farmer sitting in front of the general store, "we used to talk 'bout how much you could raise on one hundred acres—an' we meant corn, not guv'mint loans."

PUTTING THEIR LIVES ON THE LINE FOR YOU

I stopped my car at the corner of North Elm and Bellevue when I heard the siren. I looked in the direction of the noise and saw a police car approaching. The blue light on the roof was flashing and the siren blaring at a high pitch.

I watched as the police car sped by. I watched the police car disappear going west on Bellevue. I thought about the young police officer behind the wheel, and others like him. He was alone. I thought about the siren. Sirens seldom, if ever, signal good news. When you hear one somebody is usually in trouble.

We somehow have a tendency to take policemen and firemen for granted, like they come with the territory, until we need them and then it becomes a different ball of wax altogether. Yes, until we have need of their services they're just a nameless silhouette in a police car or on a fire wagon.

Unfortunately we live in a violent world where human life seems to become less and less valuable each day. People, innocent and unsuspecting people, die in random shootings. People die in the workplace, as they did in Royal Park, Michigan. Remember? A fired postal worker returned to the post office, killed four co-workers, and injured several others.

Then there was the crazy who took out his pistol and just started shooting at will in an Atlanta shopping mall. Several were killed as they sat and ate lunch in the food section.

We read where some individual holds an entire elementary classroom hostage because he's angry at his ex-wife who works in the school cafeteria.

In Brooklyn, New York, one student shoots and kills a fellow student. The next day it happens again at a different school.

A ruthless arsonist was busy almost every night for a month in Nashville, Tennessee. Each fire puts people, especially firemen and policemen, at risk.

Far too often those risks result in tragedy for those who put their lives on the line for us every day, but they respond nevertheless. Each police officer and fireman knew that when he signed on, but that doesn't make the risk any less dangerous.

I was in Nashville recently and learned something that, while it won't return a dead policeman or fireman, makes the tragedy a little easier for the surviving family. And it shows them that there are those who care and appreciate them.

Early on the morning of October 9, police lieutenant Ronnie Woodward was gunned down when he stopped a stolen car on his way home from a second job. Woodard and his wife, Becky, had recently bought a home and the second job helped with the mortgage and other bills.

Twelve years earlier, a group of Nashville businessmen and women got together and formed a club to help families of police officers and firemen killed in the line of duty.

Known as the 100 Club of Nashville, it has worked quietly and with little fanfare in helping relieve some of the worries of our public servants.

The club paid off all Woodard's debts. This amounted to more than $130,000.

To date the club has helped the families of six policemen and firemen. It has a membership of 225 and each pays $200 a year toward the assistance fund. Additionally, entertainers including Johnny Cash, George Jones, Tammy Wynette, and Waylon Jennings have helped with benefit shows.

There is now more than $788,000 in the club's assistance fund.

Let's hope and pray it's never needed.